The Chinese Exclusion Act

DOI: 10.1057/9781137339096

Also by Ben Railton

REDEFINING AMERICAN IDENTITY: From Cabeza de Vaca to Barack Obama

CONTESTING THE PAST, RECONSTRUCTING THE NATION: American Literature and Culture in the Gilded Age, 1876–1893

DOI: 10.1057/9781137339096

palgrave▸pivot

The Chinese Exclusion Act: What It Can Teach Us about America

Ben Railton

palgrave
macmillan

DOI: 10.1057/9781137339096

THE CHINESE EXCLUSION ACT

First published in 2013 by
PALGRAVE MACMILLAN®
in the United States—a division of St. Martin's Press LLC,
175 Fifth Avenue, New York, NY 10010.

Where this book is distributed in the UK, Europe and the rest of the world, this is by Palgrave Macmillan, a division of Macmillan Publishers Limited, registered in England, company number 785998, of Houndmills, Basingstoke, Hampshire RG21 6XS.

Palgrave Macmillan is the global academic imprint of the above companies and has companies and representatives throughout the world.

Palgrave® and Macmillan® are registered trademarks in the United States, the United Kingdom, Europe and other countries.

ISBN: 978-1-137-33910-2 EPUB
ISBN: 978-1-137-33909-6 PDF
ISBN: 978-1-137-33908-9 Hardback

Library of Congress Cataloging-in-Publication Data is available from the Library of Congress.

A catalogue record of the book is available from the British Library.

First edition: 2013

www.palgrave.com/pivot

DOI: 10.1057/9781137339096

For Jess, my ideal reader

DOI: 10.1057/9781137339096

Contents

DOI: 10.1057/9781137339096

Acknowledgments

For getting it all started, thanks to Chola Chisunka, the-Fitchburg State University Graduate English Colloquium series, and an audience of engaged and interested colleagues and students.

For helping me flesh it out, thanks to Shirley Wagner and my amazing group of Adult Learning in the Fitchburg Area (ALFA) students.

For very helpful readings and responses, thanks to James Fallows, Carolyn Karcher, Miles Orvell, David Palumbo-Liu, Steve Peterson, Ilene Railton, Steve Railton, Larry Rosenwald, Jonathan Silverman, Kelley Wagers, Joe Windish, and blog commenters at multiple sites.

For helping make this into the best book it could be, thanks to Chris Chappell, Sarah Whalen, and my anonymous readers at Palgrave Macmillan.

And for support throughout, especially when I needed it most, thanks to my amazing community of family and friends, and particularly to Annie and John, Mom and Dad, Aidan and Kyle, and Jess. I love you guys.

DOI: 10.1057/9781137339096

palgrave▸pivot

www.palgrave.com/pivot

Introduction: Teaching Americans the Chinese Exclusion Act

Abstract: *An overview of what better remembering the Chinese Exclusion Act can teach us about American history, culture, community, and identity: about legal and illegal immigration; about diversity and multiculturalism; and about inspiring American lives and stories, including those of the Angel Island poets, Yung Wing, and the Chinese Educational Mission students. And an argument for why such public American Studies scholarship, lessons, and arguments form a crucial part of our ongoing national narratives and conversations.*

Keywords: American identity; American Studies; Chinese Exclusion Act; public scholarship; teaching

Railton, Ben. *The Chinese Exclusion Act: What It Can Teach Us about America.* New York: Palgrave Macmillan, 2013. DOI: 10.1057/9781137339096.

In February of 2012, I had the opportunity to teach a class as part of Fitchburg State University's Adult Learning in the Fitchburg Area (ALFA) program, an initiative targeted at retired residents pursuing lifelong learning. I decided to focus my five-week syllabus on "Expanding Our Collective Memories," highlighting and analyzing American events and histories that we don't generally include in our national narratives and with which I imagined the students would not be familiar. Yet I quickly discovered that, while the course's twenty-five students were very open to learning more about American history and culture, they were also already very knowledgeable and engaged; for example, on the day when we talked about the American Indian Movement and the "Native American Renaissance," more than half of the class had watched a rerun of PBS's documentary series *We Shall Remain* on many of those same topics the night before. Much of the time, that is, I wasn't expanding their collective memories so much as contributing additional layers and contexts to some strong starting points.

There was really only one of my five main topics on which none of the students had any prior, specific perspectives: the Chinese Exclusion Act. When I polled them at the start of that class, only two of the twenty-five could recall ever having heard of the Act, and neither of those two knew anything about it other than the basic discriminatory purpose captured in the name. While I have not had the chance to poll Americans more generally on the same question, one of my fundamental premises in writing this book is that our national awareness of the Act (outside of the academic historical and Asian American communities, at least) does indeed mirror that of these ALFA students: mostly absent, with some occasional, slight recognition of the name and nothing further. Similarly, I have encountered only a few undergraduate students, in my eight years of teaching at Fitchburg State and five before that at multiple other institutions, who have heard of the Act at all, making it clear that this is not simply a generational difference or a gap that has been corrected through exposure to multicultural education.

As a nation, we don't remember the Act—not well, not even much at all; that's my first fundamental premise. My second premise is that we should, for both specific and overarching reasons. Specifically, as I detail at length in chapter 1, many of the Act's historical details and contexts are singular and striking yet at the same time exemplify ongoing and vital national trends. The 1882 Act comprised the nation's first significant immigration law, and likewise the first designation of a community of immigrants as "illegal"—making its passage both a prominent transition in our governmental and political policies and a harbinger of categories and concepts that continue to define our debates into the 21st century. However, the Act also represented the culmination of a century of evolving laws and policies related to naturalization and citizenship, shipping and transportation, ports of entry and documentation, and other issues; understanding its specifics would also help us better engage with how those policies developed alongside post-Revolutionary America itself. Moreover, the Act's most significant contemporary context and cause, the rise of xenophobic and racist narratives of a "yellow peril" threatening American society and identity, connects to a number of late 19th century themes that remain salient in our own 21st century moment: the distinct yet often overlapping interests of labor leaders and corporations, populist politicians and racist demagogues, lawmakers and media moguls; national moves toward international and imperial goals and the fears of competing and rising foreign powers that they bring with them; debates over citizenship, communal identity, and which populations and peoples are or are not entitled to those concepts and categories; and more.

While those specific historical details are thus well worth our collective engagement, I believe that a fuller national memory of the Chinese Exclusion Act would also produce overarching shifts in our narratives and communal identity. Remembering the Act, that is, and more exactly engaging with some of the American histories and stories to which it connects, would allow us to do a few very important things, would teach us the lessons that form the basis of this book's focal points and arguments. It would give us the chance to correct two wrongs, fundamentally inaccurate narratives at the core of many of our longstanding and contemporary national conversations: a wrong about the history of legal and illegal immigration, on which my first chapter's main argument focuses; and a wrong about the history of diversity and multicultural America, on which my second chapter's does. And it would give us potent examples of what has always been most right about America, in the form of the profoundly inspiring American identities and stories about which I write in my third chapter: those of the poets who carved their texts on the walls of Angel Island's holding facility; those of Yung Wing, his evolving Chinese American life and identity, and his multigenerational American family; and those of Yung's 120 students at the Chinese Educational Mission, their own Chinese American experiences and lifelong impacts, and their climactic victory on an Oakland baseball field.

DOI: 10.1057/9781137339096

In each of these ways, on its own specific terms and in its overarching implications, the Chinese Exclusion Act can help us better understand America—in our past, in our present, and in our future, and in some of the most defining and crucial elements of our national community and identity. It's important for me to make clear from the outset, however, to whom that sentence's "us" refers. After all, academic historians and scholars of immigration, law, Asian American Studies, and American culture and society are likely to be already familiar with many of these specific details, and might similarly feel as if my chapters' arguments are generally accepted and shared across these scholarly communities. Yet my third fundamental premise is that on these histories and issues, as on so many crucial American themes, there is a substantial disconnect between our scholarly awareness and perspectives and those of Americans more broadly; and, relatedly, that many of our scholarly conversations and arguments take for granted shared knowledge that is in fact not widely shared outside of our academic communities, making it difficult if not impossible for broader American audiences to connect to, learn from, and participate in those conversations.

I hope it goes without saying that I believe there to be great value to those specifically academic communities and conversations; much of my work and writing has been and will continue to be situated within them, after all. Yet I am at the same time more and more convinced of the value of—indeed the pressing need for—public American Studies scholarship, for work and writing that seeks to contribute to and impact conversations and communities at the most broad and national levels. In order to do so, scholars cannot abandon goals such as historical accuracy, analytical rigor and complexity, and engagement with those voices that have come before ours—goals that often distinguish scholarly work from partisan punditry or propaganda, and that help define the value of our ideas and contributions. But we must be willing to write about questions and themes that might feel familiar or shared within our academic communities but that are, in many cases and certainly in the cases on which this book focuses, largely unknown, if not indeed misrepresented, in our broader national conversations and narratives. When I write that "the Chinese Exclusion Act can help us better understand America," then, my "us" refers to all Americans—and this book's three chapters constitute my attempts to contribute my public scholarly perspective on and analyses of these themes and histories to national narratives and conversations that exist outside of (and, too often, separate from) academic debates.

DOI: 10.1057/9781137339096

Although we academic scholars are not always good at acknowledging or engaging with them, those national and public narratives and conversations about our histories and identities do exist—and, I would argue, often feature in leading and "expert" roles (in part because of academic scholars' reticence) voices that are far more partisan and propagandistic than scholarly. In my Conclusion I mention one of the most egregious offenders: Glenn Beck's Beck University (motto: "Learn History as It Really Happened"), and specifically its use of "historian" David Barton as the principal "scholarly" voice in classes and conversations about American history and identity (forgive the scare quotes, but to my mind Barton is at best a minister and at worst a charlatan, and neither a historian nor a scholar in any case). It might seem as if by responding to figures like Barton and Beck—or to similar figures like Sarah Palin and Pat Buchanan, with whose voices my first and second chapters open—academic and serious scholars will be lowering ourselves to their partisan level and demeaning the work that we do. But the truth, as I see it, is that if we do not respond, do not seek to add our voices to the conversations about America that are happening in our public spaces, then we cede the field entirely over to these other kinds of voices—and, more significantly, leave American audiences with no opportunity to learn and engage with histories and stories alternative to, and far more complex and nuanced and accurate than, those being created by figures like Beck, Barton, Palin, and Buchanan.

Not all Americans learn their history from such figures (although Barton's books sell millions of copies and Beck University has been popular enough to expand its offerings every year); but the simple fact is that they are going to learn it somewhere. As the recent example of Steven Spielberg's film *Lincoln* reminds us, popular culture and mass media provide another potent space for the creation and dissemination of national narratives. Spielberg's (and screenwriter Tony Kushner's) reliance upon the work of Doris Kearns Goodwin, as well as the prominent responses of historians such as Kate Masur to the film, illustrates the possibilities for public scholarly voices to join and influence our national conversations over historical figures, events, and themes. Yet while the case of *Lincoln* represents more positive connections between mass media and public scholarship, most pop culture works do not come with such scholarly accompaniment; as a result many remain far less nuanced or impressive in their engagements with our national histories. That's not their job—*Abraham Lincoln: Vampire Hunter* was written and then filmed

DOI: 10.1057/9781137339096

to entertain, and there's nothing wrong with that—but once again, the presence of such cultural engagements with history, if coupled with the absence of public scholarly contributions to our national conversations over those issues, might well produce American audiences whose awareness of their histories comes solely from such less than ideal sources.

There's one existing academic space and community that already more closely parallels such public national conversations, however: the classroom. In that space, after all, students must first learn about, understand, and engage at length and in depth with their subjects and questions, including the kinds of histories and details that their professors might take for granted in their scholarly work, before they can then develop their own analyses and arguments in response to them. In a very meaningful sense, then, I would argue that public scholarly work represents an extended form of teaching, rather than simply a reframing of our academic writing for a different audience. Indeed, just as academic language in a classroom setting succeeds only inasmuch as it communicates with the students and helps create a communal conversation, so too must public scholarly writing be judged on how it connects to our audiences and to the conversations into which we are hoping to add our voices. Which is to say, if we scholars see our public writing as a kind of teaching, in the most democratic and conversational sense of the role, it will encourage us to do in that public work all those things we strive to do for the students in our classes: make clear the value and stakes of what they're learning and doing; help them learn about, access, and connect to the histories and stories with which we're working; develop their own perspectives on and analyses of these crucial questions; and then put those ideas in conversation with ours, with each other's, and with the many other voices that have contributed and continue to contribute to America's narratives and debates.

Just as I always encourage my students to take those latter two steps, to develop their own takes on our shared materials and topics, to push beyond my starting points and see where their own responses and ideas take them, so too do I hope that my perspectives and analyses, in each chapter and on every point of this book, will be further contextualized and extended: by reading the primary sources and voices about which I write; by engaging with the arguments and analyses of the other scholars to whose works I refer in my concluding "Further Reading" section (and the many others with whom they engage, and so on); and most significantly by taking part in ongoing conversations and debates among both

DOI: 10.1057/9781137339096

academic scholars and all interested Americans. If this book can help prompt Americans to such further investigations and discussions—of the Chinese Exclusion Act's specific histories and stories, of the overarching issues and questions to which they connect, and of what they can teach us about some of the most defining ideas of who we are and why that matters—it will have achieved my highest goals for my public American Studies scholarship. And in so doing it will, as I argue in my Conclusion, likewise contribute to and offer lessons for some of our most pressing and vital 21st century conversations and debates.

DOI: 10.1057/9781137339096

1

What the Act Can Teach Us about Immigration History and Laws

Abstract: *The phrase "My ancestors came here legally," whether deployed by Sarah Palin, Colin Powell, or anonymous web commenters, represents a widely accepted yet fundamentally inaccurate understanding of the history of immigration and law in America. Remembering the Chinese Exclusion Act helps us consider the absence of national immigration laws for the first post-revolutionary century, and thus highlights the historical meaningless of concepts such as "legal immigrant" and "illegal immigrant" during that era. It also connects us to the ethnically and nationally discriminatory laws that developed from the 1882 Exclusion Act through the 1920s Quota Acts (and lasted until the 1965 Immigration Act), under which "legal" and "illegal" were still far from consistent or stable categories.*

Keywords: Chinese Exclusion Act; Ellis Island; illegal immigrants; immigration; immigration laws; legal immigrants

Railton, Ben. *The Chinese Exclusion Act: What It Can Teach Us about America.* New York: Palgrave Macmillan, 2013. DOI: 10.1057/9781137339096.

On June 1, 2011, Sarah Palin's bus tour of America arrived at Ellis Island, where the former vice presidential candidate and current media figure delivered a brief speech on the site and its connection to the history of American immigration. Palin's speeches throughout the tour were geared directly toward contemporary, contested issues and debates—an emphasis best illustrated by her revision, a few days later at a stop in Massachusetts, of the purposes of Paul Revere's ride to include support for gun ownership—and the Ellis Island speech was no exception: she used it as an opportunity to critique the DREAM Act (which was during that period being debated in Congress) and what she called its "usurping" of the American legal system.

Yet despite that explicitly contemporary and partisan component to Palin's Ellis Island remarks, in her speech's most central point she expressed a longstanding, widely shared, and indeed I would argue generally accepted American narrative: that in the past most immigrants to the United States came here legally, that it has thus always been a matter of choice whether a new arrival pursues that legal path ("stands in line and follows the rules," as Palin put it) or opts for illegal immigration instead, and that the larger numbers of late 20th and early 21st century illegal immigrants represent an increase in the community of arrivals choosing the path outside of the law. "My ancestors came here legally," goes a particularly common version of this narrative, one found again and again in letters to the editor and the comments sections of online news articles or opinion pieces related to any aspect of immigration policy or history, and even immortalized on a series of t-shirts (featuring different national flags) available for purchase at the website CafePress.com. That seemingly straightforward and factual statement is, moreover, almost always accompanied by the implicit, and indeed often explicit, follow up argument that "it's only fair that we require all current immigrants to do the same and punish those who choose not to."

In September 2011, New Hampshire Congressman Frank Guinta articulated a particularly clear version of each element of this narrative, in a piece entitled "Frankly Speaking: Illegal Immigration—Making Washington Enforce the Law" that Guinta posted on his website to explain his support for H.R. 2497, the HALT (Hinder the Administration's Legalization Temptation) Act. Guinta, who is Italian American in heritage but whose family has apparently been in the United States since at least the early 20th century, wrote "I am not opposed to legal immigration. I'm a product of it, just like many of you are. My ancestors came here legally from overseas. But illegal immigration is something entirely different. The U.S. is a nation of laws. Illegal immigrants choose not to play by the rules, and then expect to receive all the privileges given to those who followed the law and now live here legally."

Guinta's words have been echoed by other political figures and commentators on numerous occasions, as exemplified by several from just the last two years. In a 2011 series of biographical and policy statements from candidates for the Kansas State Legislature, retired Federal Judge John Rubin noted that, "I am a child and grandchild of immigrants who came to this country from Italy, Greece, and Russia in the late 19th and early 20th centuries. So I take a back seat to no one in my admiration and respect for the foreign-born immigrants of all nations and cultures who, like my ancestors, came here legally, assimilated and contributed so much to our country's strength, freedom, diversity, and economic prosperity. But they came here legally; that is the key." When Virginia legislators announced their 2011 plans for a series of anti-illegal-immigration laws, they did so with a statement that began, "House Republicans believe that playing by the rules and abiding by the law is important. Countless immigrants to this great nation have come here to embrace the American Dream, and we very much honor legal immigrants by ensuring that when people enter our country for legal purposes and they observe the rules, we welcome them. It's that simple." In articulating his support for his state's own high-profile and controversial police profiling law, S.B. 1070, Arizona State Representative Steve Montenegro, a descendant of immigrants from El Salvador, argued that, "I am saying if you came here illegally, get in line, come in the right way." And throughout the spring of 2012, in promotional appearances to publicize his memoir and expound on the presidential race and the state of American politics, former Secretary of State Colin Powell framed points about immigration reform by noting, "My parents came here 90 years ago [from Jamaica], legally I might add."

As was the case with Palin's remarks, there are of course political and partisan elements to each of these examples and their contexts: voters to sway, laws to pass, points to score. But I would argue that in each instance this particular narrative of legal and illegal immigration, the idea that both are longstanding and relatively stable historical categories (and thus in each era represent two distinct choices that individuals can and do make), is being presented as a given, a shared history outside of those political debates, something on which all Americans can

DOI: 10.1057/9781137339096

and would agree. And in case that narrative has not been sufficiently internalized by the average American, less overtly political (or at least partisan) institutions such as the Center for Immigration Studies (CIS), an independent, nonprofit research organization that has been funded in part by the U.S. Census Bureau, continue to work at reinforcing it. For example, throughout his 2006 study entitled "Two Sides of the Same Coin: The Connection Between Legal and Illegal Immigration," CIS author James R. Edwards, Jr., creates very similar narratives of the consistent and longstanding histories of and relationships between legal and illegal immigration: in broad framing ideas, such as Edwards' thesis that "when legal immigration levels have been high, illegal immigration levels have also tended to be high", and in specific historical references to the two categories, as when he writes that "an average of 520,000 legal immigrants entered each year between 1880–1890."

Given the frequency with which these narratives of the longstanding histories of legal and illegal immigration are referenced in our political arguments, policy studies, and news stories, it's no surprise that even many vocal public advocates for more immigrant-friendly policies (the DREAM Act, amnesties for undocumented immigrants already in the country, changes in the laws for new arrivals, etc.) tend to focus on arguments about our current "broken system" or on empathetic appeals to human experiences and suffering, rather than to challenge these predominant narratives and histories in any overt way. Indeed, it takes a significant effort to find any mainstream journalist, politician or public figure, or commentator willing to acknowledge, in a clear and central way, the simple and vital fact at the heart of American immigration history: for nearly all of our nation's past, from the first 16th and 17th century moments of European arrival until the mid-1920s, the categories of "legal" and "illegal" immigration did not exist, and so referring to immigrants from any and all of those periods as legal or illegal is a disingenuous and almost entirely meaningless exercise in anachronism and inaccuracy.

Academic historians and scholars tend to be familiar with these basic facts, and such familiarity can make it seem unnecessary to write about them at length (or even at all). One of this manuscript's anonymous reviewers, responding to this chapter's frame and the "My ancestors came here legally" idea, put the question to me directly: "Who is arguing that?" It's undoubtedly the case that few if any academics or scholars are doing so, and thus as viewed from within academic conversations and

DOI: 10.1057/9781137339096

communities I might seem to be responding to straw men. But Palin, Powell, and the other figures I quoted above are not made of straw; indeed, they are public and prominent voices whose words and arguments have the potential to influence many Americans and reinforce shared narratives. Moreover, I would reiterate that I see their references to the "my ancestors" concept as precisely the least controversial aspect of their ideas or perspectives, as instead an engagement with what is a widely shared and generally accepted national narrative about the histories of legal and illegal immigration (if one that each figure then uses for his or her own, often more divisive purposes). If we academic scholars do not make public our very distinct ideas about immigration history and law, we will leave that narrative unchallenged; whatever more complex and nuanced issues we analyze instead, we will thus be leaving many of our fellow Americans with a largely inaccurate sense of some of the core questions of American immigration history. And my contention in this chapter is that for those of us who seek to push back publicly on those narratives and histories, the 1882 Chinese Exclusion Act represents a particularly striking and effective starting point through which to do so.

* * *

The Chinese Exclusion Act was, in every meaningful sense, the first national immigration law. There have been national laws pertaining to citizenship for new arrivals since the Naturalization Acts of the 1790s[1]; laws dealing with basic documentation of ships and passengers coming to the United States have been on the books since the 1819 Steerage Act; and with the 1862 Anti-Coolie Act, Congress responded for the first time to a particular group of arrivals, making it illegal for certain kinds of forced Chinese labor to be imported into the country. The latter law was extended and made slightly more anti-immigrant by the 1875 Page Act; while the Act continued to regulate forced immigration (i.e., kidnapping) of "Coolies," it also allowed the federal government to prohibit immigrants in a couple of very specific categories: prostitutes,[2] and individuals convicted of and still serving their sentences for crimes (other than political ones) in their native countries. Each of these Acts certainly represents an influential and interesting part of our evolving national histories of immigration, citizenship, and government; the more we can collectively engage with all of them, the broader and deeper will be our resulting knowledge of those histories and of how they developed

DOI: 10.1057/9781137339096

alongside our national identity throughout the post-Revolutionary century. But when it comes to immigration laws, the bottom line is this: if an American's ancestors arrived in the United States prior to 1882 and weren't kidnapped Chinese laborers, prostitutes, or escaped convicts, they were subject to no national laws of any kind, and thus were neither legal nor illegal immigrants.[3]

The Chinese Exclusion Act both represented a significant shift in that history and yet still left virtually all immigrant arrivals unaffected by the law. On the one hand, the Act, which made it illegal for nearly all Chinese immigrants to enter the United States (temporary visitors such as students, merchants, and diplomats were exempt from this Act), was the first law to restrict, and indeed the first that applied to, a broad community of arrivals.[4] Initially the Act excluded Chinese arrivals only for a period of ten years, but the 1892 Geary Act extended the ban for another decade, and in 1902 a revised act established the ban as the law of the land with no horizon of expiration. In case the Act's overtly exclusionary and discriminatory function was not sufficiently apparent, a series of follow up laws and decisions thoroughly reinforced that purpose: an 1884 amendment to the Act clarified that the law applied to ethnic Chinese regardless of their country of origin (among other amplifications of the law's enforcement); the 1888 Scott Act prohibited any Chinese American who left the United States from returning; and an 1894 Act made it illegal for individuals affected by any of these laws to petition the government for redress. In at least four significant cases the Supreme Court weighed in on and sided with these laws: ruling in 1889's *Chae Chan Ping vs. United States* that the Exclusion Act and Scott Act were both constitutional; and in 1895's *United States vs. Lem Moon Sing*, 1896's *Wong Wing vs. United States*, and 1898's *United States vs. Wong Kim Ark* ruling in favor of (respectively) the ban on petitions, federal customs officers' complete and unchallengeable authority to make the decisions of restriction or admission, and the law denying readmission for those who left the country. Gradually these restrictions were apparently also applied by customs officers to arrivals from other Asian nations and communities; that practice was solidified by 1917's Immigration Act, which prohibited all arrivals from the so-called Asiatic Barred Zone (basically any South and Southeast Asian nation not "owned by the United States").

So, again, a significant shift: as of 1882 the majority of the tens of thousands of continuing Chinese arrivals to the United States[5] were now deemed illegal immigrants, and that newly meaningful—really, outside

DOI: 10.1057/9781137339096

of certain classes of criminals, newly created—national legal category would gradually be extended to other Asian immigrants over the next four decades. It would also produce the first mechanisms through which illegal arrivals skirted the law, including the complex case of the "paper sons," young Chinese men who in the aftermath of the 1906 San Francisco fire (which destroyed many immigration records at the Angel Island station) forged papers stating familial relationships with Chinese Americans in order to gain entry to the United States. Yet despite this striking change for certain immigrant communities, for any other arrival (outside of those aforementioned criminal classes and other socially outcast categories such as "lunatics"), anyone coming to the United States from another region or nation—as of 1882, anywhere besides China; as of 1920, still many parts of Asia (such as the Philippines, Turkey, and the Middle East) and all of Europe, Africa, Australia and the South Pacific, and Latin and South America—this law did not apply to them, and hence did not change their situation at all. That is, I am arguing, it did not render them suddenly legal immigrants—the fact that Chinese (and eventually other Asian) immigrants were now excluded by law, after all, did not address in any sense the issue of immigrants from other nations and regions. These other immigrants were no more legal or illegal than they had been prior to the Exclusion Act; they were simply immigrant arrivals, ones outside of any legal restriction or categorization.

As this is one of the more significant points of my arguments here, I want to push on it for a moment more. Certainly it would be possible to argue that doing something in the absence of any legal restrictions (or indeed laws of any kind) is doing something "legally," but I don't believe that's how the term is generally (if ever) used or meant. Would we say that we're "breathing legally," just because there are no laws making it illegal?[6] If breathing were made illegal for only those in a certain community (people who have been exposed to and thus might exhale poisonous gases, for example), would we then describe everyone else as "legal breathers"? To my mind, the answer to both questions is clearly "no"—that the only way it makes sense to describe an action as "legal" or "illegal" is if the law applies to those taking the action, if an individual and his or her actions exist under that law's jurisdiction. Again, for all other (noncriminal) immigrants during these decades after the Exclusion Act's passage, there remained no immigration laws that applied to them. And to put that crucial fact in relationship to one other defining thread of our national narratives, the argument that so frequently follows the phrase "my ancestors

DOI: 10.1057/9781137339096

came here legally" (and that is to my mind implied by the phrase whether it is explicitly stated or not): those other immigrants certainly did not "choose" any aspect of their status, no more than a Chinese immigrant could "choose" whether or not he or she was subject to the Exclusion Act; the idea of "choice" simply continues to have no meaningful connection to the realities of immigration, law, and identity during this period.

It was not, indeed, until the early 1920s, in response to World War I–inspired fears of sedition and anarchism, the ongoing "Red Scare," reinvigorated anti-Catholic bigotry, and other complex influences, that Congress passed immigration laws that genuinely encompassed most arrivals to the United States. That shift began with the 1921 Emergency Quota Law, which established temporary annual quotas for most immigrants based on their country of birth; the quotas were set at 3 percent of the number of foreign-born persons from each nation recorded on the 1910 Census. And three years later, the landmark 1924 Immigration Act (also known as the Johnson-Reed Act) made such immigration policy the ongoing law of the land, in two stages: a particularly retrograde and exclusionary first period, with quotas for the next three years based on 2 percent of each nation's foreign-born population on the 1890 Census; and a more contemporarily grounded yet still broadly limiting second period, with the overall immigrant quota for every year after 1927 being set at 150,000 and divided up by the national origins of the overall U.S. population on the 1920 Census.

As a result of these laws, after 1924 most immigrants to the United States could indeed be categorized, for the first time in our history, as legal (if they were part of their year of arrival's established quota for their nation) or illegal (if the quota had been met and they continued to enter the United States). Yet it would still be far from accurate to describe these circumstances as a consistent set of "rules" that all potential immigrants could choose either to follow or to disregard. For one thing, the Chinese Exclusion Act and its subsequent Asian extensions remained in place for all those prospective arrivals. For another, the quota numbers were so drastically different as to remain nothing short of exclusionary for many arrivals: many nations, including Greece, Turkey, and Egypt, received the legal minimum quota of 100 immigrants per year; others, such as Spain at 131 and Australia at 121, were not far beyond the minimum. And all these circumstances were of course not in any way a matter of "choice" for any immigrant, but rather a reflection of a continued reliance on national and ethnic discrimination as the grounding for our laws and policies.

DOI: 10.1057/9781137339096

Those exclusionary and discriminatory purposes to the 1920s laws were revealed most clearly in the Congressional debates over them. For example, South Carolina Senator Ellison DuRant Smith argued in a speech in support of the 1924 act, "It seems to me the point as to this measure...is that the time has arrived when we should shut the door....Thank God we have in America perhaps the largest percentage of any country in the world of the pure, unadulterated Anglo-Saxon stock,...and it is for the preservation of that splendid stock that has characterized us that I would make this not an asylum for the oppressed of all countries, but a country to assimilate and perfect that splendid type of manhood." Ironically, it was in response to the one less exclusionary element of the 1924 Act—the provision that immigrants from "independent nations" in the Western Hemisphere were not subject to its quotas[7]—that Congressman John Box advanced an even more explicitly discriminatory argument about that Act's purposes, in a 1928 speech calling for an end to Mexican immigration. Box began his speech by arguing that "every reason which calls for the exclusion of the most wretched, ignorant, dirty, diseased, and degraded people of Europe or Asia demands that the illiterate, unclean, peonized masses moving this way from Mexico be stopped at the border"; while many of his peers might not have used that list of extreme adjectives to describe immigrants, it's fair to say that more might have agreed with his later statement that one "purpose of the immigration laws is the protection of American racial stock from further degradation or change through mongrelization." At the very least, the quotas at the core of the 1920s Acts were designed precisely in an effort to exclude those arrivals thought to be less desirable (for whatever reason), putting such discriminatory categorizations at the heart of the first broad definitions of legal and illegal immigration.

It was not until the 1940s and the legal responses to World War II, such as the 1943 Magnuson Act (which repealed elements of the Chinese Exclusion Act to allow Chinese war refugees to enter the United States) and the 1946 Alien Fiancées and Fiancés Act (which allowed spouses of American military members to enter outside of the quota system), that some of these policies and their accompanying legal definitions would begin to shift. And it was only with the watershed 1965 Immigration and Nationality Act (also known as the Hart-Cellar Act) that the nationality-based quota system would be abolished and replaced by preferences based on factors such as skills and family relationships, categories that were (whatever their limitations) not at all directly tied to particular nations or regions. Subsequent laws, including the 1986 Immigration Reform and Control Act, have continued to shape our immigration policies and regulations, but that basic shift, from national/ethnic preferences to other categories, has largely remained in place. Yet it is worth emphasizing, as another corrective to many of our prominent national narratives of immigration history, just how recent such nondiscriminatory legal definitions are. That is, if it is crucial for us first to remember that only since the 1920s have the categories of legal and illegal immigration had any meaning at all for most immigrant arrivals, it is just as significant to note that for less than fifty years have those categories been applied with any across-the-board equitability and fairness to all arrivals, irrespective of their country of origin.

So what would it mean if all Americans were more aware of these facts and details, of the stages of American immigration and its laws as they have evolved over the centuries? First, to reiterate my most central point, any narrative of our immigration history—collectively or for any particular individual, family, and ancestry—that includes the categories of legal and illegal immigration prior to 1882, and virtually any one that includes them prior to 1921 and 1924 (other than for the Asian immigrants affected by the Exclusion Act and its aftermath), is fundamentally inaccurate, based on a lack of knowledge about the absence of laws affecting most immigrant arrivals for most of our nation's history. "My ancestors came here legally" has no meaning if they came before 1882 ("My ancestors were not obviously prostitutes or convicted criminals" would work in that case), and still none if they came before 1921 and were not from an Asian nation ("My ancestors were not the subject of blatant, targeted legal discrimination" would be fine).

Second, and nearly as important when it comes to the ramifications of many of these arguments, is what this increased awareness would mean for the concept of "choice" to which the argument "my ancestors came here legally" is almost always connected. That is, any narrative of immigration that deals with arrivals prior to 1965—most clearly prior to 1921, but even during the 1921–1965 period—and that treats the difference between legal and illegal immigration as a matter of choice, of how different arrivals responded to the same (or even similar) circumstances, rules, or possibilities, is likewise disconnected from the realities. Those advancing such narratives must recognize and engage with the fact that every significant immigration law prior to 1965, including those 1920s ones that did for the first time encompass most new arrivals to the United

DOI: 10.1057/9781137339096

States, was designed and intended to discriminate explicitly between different nationalities and communities. In response to such laws and the vastly varied circumstances they created, the "choices" for those different groups were likewise hugely distinct; while it's certainly interesting and important to consider what choices individuals, families, and communities made, it is entirely inaccurate and disingenuous to suggest that the "choice" between legal and illegal immigration was in any period prior to 1965 (in those few decades and situations for which it was a possibility at all) a straightforward or universal one.

Better understanding these evolving pre-1965 histories and periods of immigration and the law would also lead to a significantly more accurate and meaningful perspective on the process of arrival and entrance for immigrants during those periods. Prior to 1855, there was no national immigration arrival point of any kind; different states had different mechanisms for greeting and documenting arrivals, although with laws such as the 1819 Steerage Act Congress began to standardize some of those procedures (such as requiring customs officers to count immigrants and note their points of origin). But for the most part new arrivals during these centuries had to do little other than (at most) state their name and country of origin to the authorities on their ship or at their port of entrance. That is, for the nations and communities that sent hundreds upon hundreds of thousands of immigrants to the United States prior to the mid-19th century—England, of course, but also Ireland, Scotland, Germany (not yet a unified nation, so more exactly various states within it), France, the Netherlands, and many other Northern and Western European nations—there were not only no laws governing their admission or entrance, but also virtually no "rules" for that process. This latter point is particularly salient given the frequent fallback argument for those who claim their ancestors were legal immigrants: at the very least, such arguments often go, "my ancestors waited in line and followed the rules"; but the reality is that there were no consistent (and certainly no arduous) rules across these centuries, not least because there were no locations to which most immigrants arrived.

The 1855 opening of New York's Castle Garden Emigrant Landing Depot, in the Battery area of Lower Manhattan, provided the United States with its first official immigration station, a center for receiving and documenting immigrant arrivals. For the next thirty-five years, most of the passenger ships arriving on the east coast docked at Castle Garden, allowing for its records to trace more consistently and accurately some

DOI: 10.1057/9781137339096

basic identifying information for those arrivals: most commonly their names and nationalities, but also for many their sex, occupation, and destination within the united States. These immigrants were still not subject to any laws (since the Chinese arrivals affected by the Exclusion Act, once it was passed in 1882, came to ports on the west coast), but in the later years of this period they were ostensibly, at the time of documentation, checked for obvious signs of the kinds of excluding factors (criminal history, insanity) I mentioned above. So it's possible to say that the immigrants who came through Castle Garden "followed the rules," by allowing their basic information (or rather whatever they chose or were linguistically able to tell the authorities) to be documented and later by allowing for those cursory examinations; but it seems quite clear to me that those Americans who advance narratives like "in the past, immigrants followed the rules" mean a great deal more than stating their names or being briefly observed for obvious signs of insanity or criminal behavior.

Ellis Island, the much more famous official immigration station that replaced Castle Garden and served as the east coast center from 1892 to 1954, amplified but did not to my mind significantly change that process. As Sarah Palin's visit and remarks illustrate, Ellis has become in many cases the symbol of precisely the "my ancestors came here legally" narrative—its procedures and lines representing those past "legal" immigrants "following the rules." Yet for Ellis Island's first thirty years of operation, until the 1921 and 1924 Acts, its arriving immigrants were generally subject to no laws; Angel Island in San Francisco, which opened in 1910, became the first west coast hub and served as the principal site of the Chinese Exclusion Act's ongoing restrictions and detentions. And even Ellis Island's procedures and lines were not significantly different from those of Castle Garden: arriving immigrants did have to answer, to the best of their ability and with whatever honesty and accuracy they chose, a series of twenty-nine basic questions, both to provide that same minimal information for documentation (name, nationality, sex, and so on) and as a way of checking for some of those excluded characteristics (dangerous infectious diseases; criminal activity; "Anarchist" tendencies; etc.). But once again I would argue that these basic experiences do not at all encompass what the oft-cited idea of "following the rules" typically implies. Virtually none of the 21st century Americans making that argument, that is, would be satisfied if all currently illegal immigrant arrivals could enter the country officially by simply answering a list of questions

DOI: 10.1057/9781137339096

about their identity, background, and health—and after the Ellis Island arrivals did so, not by "choice" but because their ship had docked there, they were (until the 1920s at least) free to enter the United States, still outside of any legal category. Since an estimated 40 percent of current U.S. citizens can trace their ancestry to at least one Ellis Island arrival, it's hard to overstate how significant a more accurate perspective on what this process entailed—and what it still did not, particularly in terms of the law—would be for our national narratives and conversations.

Moreover, while the Ellis Island arrivals did have to go through those shared, if minimal, experiences and procedures, throughout much of the same period immigrants coming across either of the national borders were subject to no consistent documentation or process of any kind. The border between Canada and the United States, which my great-grandfather Albert Railton and his family crossed in the mid-1910s when they moved from Canada to New Hampshire, was until the 1920s largely unstaffed except at significant ports on either coast; the relatively minimal increase in border coverage in the 1920s was partly the result of the decade's new immigration laws, but was driven more fully by worries about illegal alcohol smuggling during Prohibition. Similarly, the Mexican border was almost entirely unmonitored until 1915, when a special group of between 50 and 100 mounted inspectors were commissioned to watch for illegal Chinese immigrants; that small and focused group was the first version of the full United States Border Patrol, which was established alongside the new Immigration Act in 1924. But even that Patrol numbered only around 450 officers for its first couple decades, meaning that much of the Mexican border, like the Canadian one, remained largely open to immigrant arrivals until at least the post–World War II era. Again, these details provide a more full and accurate picture of our immigration history in these periods, but they do more than that: they make clear that different immigrant experiences, especially in the centuries prior to the 1920s but even well beyond them, varied widely, and they illustrate that the procedures, rules, and laws under which those different immigrants arrived in the United States were similarly hugely distinct, from each other and (even more fully and more saliently for our current debates) from our contemporary policies and laws.

None of that is to imply that American attitudes toward immigration prior to the Chinese Exclusion Act and the even more broadly discriminatory 1920s laws had always been entirely open or welcoming. Quite the opposite, in fact—each major historical wave of immigrant

DOI: 10.1057/9781137339096

arrivals had produced explicit, public, xenophobic responses, and corresponding arguments in favor of limiting immigration. In Ben Franklin's 1751 *Observations Concerning the Increases of Mankind, Peopling of Countries, etc.*, the already prominent Philadelphian and future Founding Father responded to a wave of German immigration into his home state by asking "Why should the *Palatine Boors* [natives of a particular German region] be suffered to swarm into our Settlements, and by herding together establish their Language and Manners to the Exclusion of ours? Why should Pennsylvania, founded by the *English*, become a Colony of Aliens, who will shortly be so numerous as to Germanize us instead of our Anglifying them, and will never adopt our Language or Customs, any more than they can acquire our Complexion?" A wave of French arrivals toward the end of the 18th century, paired with an undeclared military conflict with that nation, greatly contributed to the first genuinely controversial federal laws, the 1798 Alien and Sedition Acts, which (until they were reversed) both narrowed the possibilities for citizenship and connected these new immigrants to fears of rebellion and treason. And most famously, the wave of Irish immigrants who fled the Potato Famine between 1845 and 1855 produced the Know Nothing Party, the first significant American political party or movement founded in direct opposition to immigration; the Party's inaugural 1856 platform began with the assertion that "Americans must rule America," and went on to argue for significant changes to American naturalization and citizenship laws, among other methods of discouraging immigrant arrivals.

Recognizing this history of xenophobic opposition to immigration adds a few more elements to the revised, more accurate narrative for which I'm arguing here. Certainly it illustrates the silliness of such worries: Pennsylvania did not become a new German state; the Franco-American community did not seditiously plot to overthrow the United States; and Irish immigrants became a much more positive and meaningful presence in and part of America than the Know Nothings ever were. But this history can also reinforce two of the most salient, and again under-narrated, features of our immigration laws. First, it reminds us that there were no immigration laws of any kind operating in these earlier periods—hence the worries expressed by figures in each period about what that absence of laws or restrictions, and the concurrent opportunity for arrivals from these nations to immigrate freely and fully, might mean for our community and future. And second, this history

DOI: 10.1057/9781137339096

reveals the more complex but even more significant fact that arguments in favor of immigration laws have almost always been directly tied to xenophobic attitudes toward particular immigrant arrivals and communities. That is, it's no coincidence that the first national immigration law was the Chinese Exclusion Act, and it's similarly unsurprising that the first broadly encompassing laws were the 1920s quota-establishing ones. Despite historical complexities and shifts, our debates over and moves toward immigration laws have consistently been driven not simply by desires for regulation or fairness or the like, but precisely by the goal of creating the category of illegal immigration in specific and discriminatory ways, of restricting and excluding certain groups based entirely on who they were and where they were from.

It's important to add that the histories of naturalization and citizenship, while at times (as in the case of the Alien and Sedition Acts) overlapping quite directly with these kinds of xenophobic fears, also represent a distinct series of laws, one with a much longer and more multipart history than that of our immigration laws. The U.S. Constitution is entirely silent on immigration—a notable absence, since Franklin's 1751 text makes clear that the issue was part of our national conversations by that time; whatever we make of that absence, it at least highlights in yet another way the absence of national immigration laws.[8] On the other hand, the Constitution explicitly designates to Congress the power to establish a "uniform rule of naturalization"; beginning in the following decade, with the Naturalization Acts of 1790, 1795, 1798, Congress did just that. Although those laws have certainly evolved over the centuries since—most prominently with the 14th Amendment's clarification of the concept of "birthright citizenship," an idea that has become intertwined with anti-immigration sentiments through current debates over "anchor babies"—they have thus been a part of our national legal and social fabrics since our political origins. So it's certainly possible that when someone argues that "my ancestors came here legally," he or she is referring to those ancestors' efforts to gain citizenship, a process that is of course unavailable to contemporary illegal immigrants (and that, not coincidentally, was likewise made impossible for any and all Chinese Americans by the Chinese Exclusion Act). But again, laws dealing with naturalization and citizenship are distinct from those addressing immigrants at their moment of arrival, and recognizing both kinds will allow us to narrate their respective histories and realities with much more accuracy and salience.

DOI: 10.1057/9781137339096

So to come back to the most significant histories and realities on which I'm focused in this chapter: if your ancestors immigrated to the United States prior to 1882 (as did my paternal grandmother's, from Germany), they weren't legal or illegal, as there were no immigration laws to which they were subject. If they immigrated between 1882 and 1921 (as did my paternal grandfather's, from Canada; and all my maternal grandparents', from Russia and the Ukraine) and weren't coming from China or (eventually) other affected Asian nations, they still weren't legal or illegal, as those newly created restrictive laws didn't apply to them. If they came through Ellis Island during that period, they did have to answer some questions and verify that they weren't dying of a communicable illness or hoping to marry multiple women or the like; but they were still neither legal nor illegal, and didn't have to follow any "rules" outside of that basic information-providing. If they immigrated after 1921 or 1924, they were in most cases subject to the quotas established in those laws, and thus probably were legal or illegal immigrants; but even for these groups it's worth being very clear about a couple of related facts: they didn't "choose" their legality, but rather had it determined entirely by the discriminatory approach to their nation and region of origin comprised by the quotas; and their experiences were likewise drastically different if they arrived at a site like Ellis Island or crossed the (still largely unregulated) northern or southern borders. To put it succinctly: the "my ancestors came here legally" narrative has no meaning for any immigrants prior to 1882, virtually none for any prior to 1921, and is still in need of significant complication and revision for any who came prior to 1965.

"So what?," you might ask. What's the benefit of remembering these details and histories? For one thing, understanding and engaging with our collective American history more accurately, as a national community, is a significant goal in its own right, and an outcome toward which I believe all public Americanist scholars should and do work. That's true of just about any aspect of our history, doubly true for any aspect that has been present across our centuries of existence, and exponentially truer still when it comes to an issue like immigration, one that has been so defining and constitutive of our national community and identity. Getting right the basic facts about the history of American immigration, much less understanding that history's complex and evolving realities, is the equivalent of developing a shared and genuine communal understanding of the Declaration of Independence and the Constitution: it's a civic expression of core communal experiences, an act of genuine

DOI: 10.1057/9781137339096

patriotism through which we do justice to the histories and stories out of which our nation has been created, changed, and strengthened over its many centuries of existence. Such understanding and engagement, to be clear, depends on each American not only to listen to what public scholars have to say, but also and most importantly to learn more for him or herself, to look into those histories and stories and see what new perspectives that investigation yields.

Yet there's a reason why I started this chapter with Palin and the other contemporary and largely political voices I quoted there: these more accurate and complex understandings would likewise dramatically affect our contemporary and ongoing debates over issues of and related to immigration. As those voices reflect, time and again political positions on extreme and draconian anti-illegal immigration laws and policies—such as those created by the Virginia legislators I quoted, or the Arizona law supported by Representative Montenegro, or the widespread deportation efforts that the Obama administration has extended and amplified from its predecessor's policies—are tied directly to rhetorical contrasts between current illegal immigrants and those past "legal" immigrants who "chose to follow the rules." The same trend can be found in arguments in opposition to the DREAM Act, to amnesty or work programs for illegal immigrants, to social programs that (like Virginia's Bright Stars educational program for disadvantaged kids and families, in which my mother works) offer aid to illegal immigrant families (among other Americans)—it's too bad that these folks have to suffer, the arguments go, but if they had just chosen to follow the rules and immigrate legally, as those centuries of past legal immigrants did, they wouldn't be facing the same problems. (I'm leaving aside the more overtly xenophobic arguments that portray illegal immigrants as diseased, as criminals, as leeches draining our nation, but those arguments likewise often if not always depend on such contrasts with other immigrants and Americans.)

Is it possible to make arguments for anti-illegal immigration legislation and policies and deportations, or in opposition to the DREAM Act and amnesty and social programs, without relying on these inaccurate histories and narratives? Of course—these are complex issues, with a variety of factors and effects, and demand serious and extended debate. But we can't begin to have those debates in meaningful ways until we move beyond the inaccurate histories, until we do away with the false and disingenuous use of terms like "legal" and "illegal immigration," "choice" and "following the rules." Once we've done that, we'll be much

DOI: 10.1057/9781137339096

better equipped to understand where we've been, to deal with the specifics of our current laws and period (both on their own terms and in relationship to those earlier ones), and to move forward as a national community engaged with—rather than relying on mistaken narratives of—our history and identity. Public scholars have a significant role to play in helping us move beyond those inaccurate histories and toward the more strong and meaningful ones. And one effective means through which we can do so is to highlight just how much the Chinese Exclusion Act can teach us about American immigration histories and laws.

Notes

1 Interestingly, the 1870 Naturalization Act, an element of Federal Reconstruction that naturalized Africans and their descendants living in the United States, purposefully did not include Asian Americans in its purview (limiting its effects to "white persons and persons of African descent"), despite the urging of Senators Charles Sumner and Lyman Trumbull that it do so. That detail makes clear both the era's rising xenophobic and nativist sentiments (which contributed directly to the Exclusion Act) and the ways in which naturalization debates have often paralleled questions of immigration and restriction; calling the Exclusion Act the first national immigration law, as I do here, should not prohibit us from recognizing and analyzing such earlier and ongoing links. I am indebted to the aforementioned anonymous reviewer for the connection to the 1870 Act.

2 Many historians believe that this provision was directed more broadly at single Chinese women; the vast majority of early Chinese arrivals had been men, and a part of the decade's fears of the "yellow peril" was the idea that women would join those men and start to create more settled American families as a result. This interpretation would certainly make the Page Act a more direct predecessor to the Chinese Exclusion Act, but does not change my broader point about the specificity of the targets of these early laws.

3 Some states did during this pre-1882 era have laws related to particular classes of arrivals, such as free blacks in many Southern states; in my analysis those laws were passed in response to and tended to focus much more on internal American migration rather than on immigration, and they were not at all consistent across different states, but they could be added to this paragraph's lists. For a contrasting argument that these state laws do in fact constitute a prior history of national immigration law, see Gerald Neuman, "The Lost Century of American Immigration Law," *Columbia Law Review* 93 (1993): 1833, 1889.

DOI: 10.1057/9781137339096

4 The full text of the brief Act is available at this website (among others): https://www.mtholyoke.edu/acad/intrel/chinex.htm.

5 The 1880 census reported just over 105,000 Chinese Americans; the 1890 census reported about 60,000 more, which means either that they all came in the two years prior to the Exclusion Act or (more likely) that at least some of them came after it was implemented.

6 There are, of course, bumper sticker slogans such as "Think: It isn't illegal yet." While I take the point of those sayings, I don't believe, in the absence of such restrictive laws, that anyone would describe him or herself as "thinking legally." Moreover, to connect this idea to the argument with which I conclude this paragraph, it would be nonsensical in the absence of such laws to claim "I choose to think legally."

7 A provision, it's worth noting, that renders Colin Powell's aforementioned point about his parents' "legal" arrival from Jamaica in the 1920s as inaccurate as most other such statements.

8 Article I, Section 9 does allow the importation of slaves to continue until 1808, when it would be (and was) outlawed. But to my mind the slave trade is an entirely separate issue from immigration, for obvious reasons.

DOI: 10.1057/9781137339096

2

What the Act Can Teach Us about Diversity

Abstract: *While opinions differ widely on our contemporary emphases on a diverse and multicultural American society, there is widespread agreement that it was with the 1965 Immigration Act that the nation's demographics, community, and identity began to change dramatically in those ways. Yet the Chinese Exclusion Act can help connect us to longstanding American histories and communities that reveal the opposite: that our nation has been hugely diverse and multicultural from its origin points; and that the shift toward a less diverse society was produced by limiting and discriminatory laws such as the Exclusion Act and the 1920s Quota Acts. That somewhat less diverse America was the change and aberration, and our contemporary diversity represents a return to a founding American identity.*

Keywords: American identity; Asian Americans; Chinese Exclusion Act; diversity; Mexican Americans; multiculturalism

Railton, Ben. *The Chinese Exclusion Act: What It Can Teach Us about America.* New York: Palgrave Macmillan, 2013. DOI: 10.1057/9781137339096.

On May 1, 2007, two weeks after the shocking and brutal massacre of over thirty students and teachers at Virginia Tech, former Republican presidential candidate and current conservative commentator Pat Buchanan published a column on the shooting. The national responses to and conversations about the massacre had already begun to shift away from shared shock and horror and sympathies and toward more divisive and partisan topics, with most of those debates centering on issues of gun control and violence—questions of whether a defeated Virginia law to allow students to carry guns on campus would have helped avert the massacre, of how the shooter (Cho Seung-Hui) had been able to obtain his semi-automatic handgun despite a documented history of mental illness, and the like. But while Buchanan addresses those debates in his opening two paragraphs, the thrust of his arguments is very different, and is reflected in his column's title: "The Dark Side of Diversity."

From the opening sentence of his third paragraph—"Almost no attention has been paid to the fact that Cho Seung-Hui was not an American at all, but an immigrant, an alien"—Buchanan's extreme, xenophobic, and bigoted take on the Virginia Tech shooter and his significance is stated clearly and directly. And I should similarly state clearly from the outset here that I am not seeking to attribute most of Buchanan's repellent views to any significant percentage of his fellow Americans, and am certainly not arguing that those views represent in their totality widely shared national narratives. Buchanan calls the Immigration Act of 1965 "the greatest invasion in our history"; says of those who immigrated after that law that "almost all [are] from countries whose peoples have never fully assimilated in any Western country"; and then, in his most extended, central, and logically nonsensical section, details precisely what he means by diversity's "dark side," arguing for a "correlation ... between mass migrations and mass murder" by highlighting a motley baker's dozen of entirely disparate and unconnected cases (from the previous five decades of American life) in which prominent crimes have been committed by immigrants or the second or third generation children of immigrants. Such positions are deeply representative of Buchanan's own worldview, broadly if hyperbolically representative of the xenophobic strain of anti-immigrant thought I discussed in Chapter 1, and not at all representative, I firmly believe, of most Americans' perspectives.

Yet with that said, I would still argue that Buchanan's piece is grounded in a pair of interconnected narratives of American history that are much more widely shared, including by many Americans who would disagree with Buchanan on (among most other things) the meaning of those same narratives. The first is that the Immigration Act of 1965 effected a significant shift in our national community and identity, that America has become a significantly more diverse nation, with many more national and ethnic presences than ever before, as a result of the Act's policies and aftermath. When Buchanan refers alliteratively to the America created by the Act and its effects as a "multicultural, multiracial, multiethnic, multilingual mammoth mall of a nation," he clearly (even leaving aside his piece's overall arguments) intends for those adjectives to be read sarcastically, as symptoms of the problem he's hoping to diagnose. But Americans at the other end of the spectrum on this issue, those who would see Buchanan's first four adjectives, and especially "multicultural," as capturing some of the best qualities of our contemporary nation, would often likewise characterize those qualities as having been dramatically amplified and deepened by the Immigration Act of 1965.

The second shared historical narrative follows directly from that sense of post-1965 shifts, although it is often left unstated or at least mostly unexplored by those arguing for such changes. If multicultural diversity has dramatically risen over the last half-century, then it stands to reason that for much of its history before this period, and certainly at its origin points, America was substantially less diverse, was in fact more culturally (racially, ethnically) homogeneous. Once again, Buchanan articulates this narrative very explicitly: "Before 1970, we were a people, a community, a country.... And as Americans no longer share the old ties of history, heritage, faith, language, tradition, culture, music, myth or morality, how can immigrants share those ties?" As with the first shared narrative, obviously many Americans would disagree with Buchanan's follow up analysis that these changes have been "alienating" (or that they are in any way a bad thing), and with his idea that we were at our best when we were more unified in those ways; likewise his connection of the prior, more homogeneous (unnamed but clearly white Anglo-Saxon Christian) culture to "morality" reinforces the hierarchies between different cultures on which Buchanan's arguments depend. Yet when it comes to the core narrative here, that America was originally and for centuries thereafter more culturally homogeneous than the multiculturally diverse nation it has become and is still becoming, I do believe that many Americans would share that perspective on our history and identity.

One way to exemplify the widespread acceptance of that narrative is to compare the melting pot and salad bowl metaphors for American culture

DOI: 10.1057/9781137339096

and community. In its earliest forms, the melting pot metaphor applied equally to all American arrivals and cultures—when French essayist Hector St. John de Crevecoeur, in one of the many pieces collected in his *Letters from an American Farmer* (1782), answered the question "What is an American?," he did so by writing in part that "Here individuals of all races are melted into a new race of man, whose labors and posterity will one day cause great changes in the world." Yet I would argue that throughout the 19th and 20th centuries the melting pot narrative evolved, and became more and more an image of every *other* race and culture being remade into (at least an approximation of) the originating, homogeneous white Anglo culture of Buchanan's historical argument. So thoroughly did this shift occur that by 1915 cultural critic Horace Kallen could famously write that "the general notion, 'Americanization,' appears to denote the adoption of English speech [and to] connote a transmutation by the 'miracle of assimilation' of Jews, Slavs, Poles, Frenchmen, Germans, Hindus, Scandinavians into beings similar in background, tradition, outlook, and spirit to the descendants of the British colonists, the Anglo-Saxon stock." Kallen's critique of that melting pot ideal as fundamentally opposed to democracy was and remains controversial; but I believe that most Americans, then and even now, would concur with that general notion of what "Americanization" has meant throughout our history.

It's precisely because even those Americans critical of the Anglifying melting pot narrative have tended to see it as the traditional core image of Americanization that proponents of post-1960s multiculturalism came up with a new metaphor for this new America: the salad bowl, a collection of different ingredients that mostly retain their original flavor yet combine to make an even more appetizing whole. Virtually all advocates for this new image have not sought to extend it back to America's historical origins, or even in any overt way into the 19th or early 20th centuries; they have instead generally argued that while the melting pot metaphor might have been an apt one for an earlier America, it cannot apply to this late 20th and early 21st century, post-1965, significantly diversified multicultural nation. Whether we entirely agree with such proponents of contemporary multicultural diversity (as I do), see them as advocating an alienating and dangerous division (as does Buchanan), or take any position in between, the fact remains that the salad bowl metaphor is indeed usually a contemporary, rather than a historical, narrative. None of those positions fundamentally challenges the widely shared narrative

DOI: 10.1057/9781137339096

of a significantly more homogeneous originating American culture and community.

There would seem to be an obvious and incontrovertible challenge to that narrative, one captured by the title of Gary Nash's multiedition American history textbook: *Red, White, and Black: The Peoples of Early North America*. After all, Native American nations and tribes have been in America since prior to any other contemporary culture's arrival, and members of African cultures arrived very shortly after the first European immigrants, such as with the first slave ship's 1619 landing in Virginia. Yet just as Buchanan is clearly able to elide those other cultures in his emphasis on a homogeneous (and, again, presumably white) originating American culture, so too I would argue does this widely shared national narrative find ways to maintain its definition alongside an awareness of these other foundational cultural presences. Sometimes that means seeing these other cultures as occupying a space outside of mainstream "America"; or recognizing their presence within it but defining it as always a conflicted and subsidiary presence; or delineating the many ways in which these cultures have constantly responded to and been defined through the dominant white culture; or using the melting pot metaphor to argue that members of these cultures have had the choice either to melt into the mainstream American culture (as best they can) or face exclusion and potential extinction. But in any case, American narratives have long found ways to acknowledge Native and African American presences while still returning to national definitions based on a homogeneous culture. Similarly, if more positively for these other originating cultures, many proponents of a post-1965 multicultural America would argue that it has coincided with and contributed to a rise in cultural awareness, power, and pride for Native Americans and African Americans as well as for the members of other immigrant communities.

So despite the many different and even opposed contemporary political and social positions on topics like multiculturalism and diversity, I believe that there is widespread American agreement that our nation is significantly more diverse today than at any earlier point in our history. While it can be difficult to find precise statements of that perspective in our public conversations, it's certainly possible to locate numerous parallel narratives that echo Buchanan's central argument: that the Immigration Act of 1965 represented a significant shift, indeed a sea-change, for American society and identity. Many of the most such overt

DOI: 10.1057/9781137339096

narratives likewise echo Buchanan's negative take on those shifts; it's in that vein, for example, that the lobbyist organization NumbersUSA ("For Lower Immigration Levels") offers on its website a piece entitled "Our National Tradition, Until the 1965 Congress Drastically Changed the Rules." The piece's (and the organization's) ostensible focus is on a more specific and less controversial shift, the increase in "numbers" of immigrants after the 1965 Act, although even that change is less dramatic than the piece claims: when converted into a percentage of the nation's population, the post-1965 waves of immigration correlate closely with earlier waves, and mostly contrast only with the much more broadly restrictive period after the 1920s quota-establishing laws. But in any case, the titular phrase "national tradition" makes clear the authors' ultimate purpose: to argue for these post-1965 changes as a radical departure from our historical identity and community.

That position on the post-1965 changes can also be found in other much more objective journalistic and public scholarly accounts. In a 2006 NPR piece, offered as context for ongoing Congressional debates over illegal immigration and immigration laws more generally, reporter Jennifer Ludden calls the 1965 law "a radical break with previous policy" that "has led to profound demographic changes in America." To bolster her arguments, she cites multiple public scholars, including UC Santa Barbara historian Otis Graham and Customs and Immigration Services historian Marian Smith. Yet both in her own writing and in her use of these historians, Ludden effects a couple of subtle but significant slippages very common to this narrative. First, she details the 1965 law's unquestionable changes in policy, but does not delineate that those changes were only to the prior four decades of laws (since the restrictive 1920s acts), rather than to an originating American tradition; the phrase "radical break," indeed, implies instead that the post-1965 openness was something entirely new to American society. And second, she pays particular attention to the post-1965 increase in the numbers of arriving immigrants, many from particular regions and nations that had been excluded during those four decades (Graham for example is quoted on the question of whether the law's framers were lying or mistaken when they argued it would not increase immigration); but she frames that increase not as an amplification or extension of existing diversity, nor as a return to a previously diverse nation after the era of the quota-driven restrictions, but instead as a "profound demographic change," a societal parallel to the law's "radical break" in policy. The 2006 Congressional

DOI: 10.1057/9781137339096

immigration debates did tend to break down into those who narrated post-1965 changes as a positive force and those who did not; but the absence of voices arguing that what had happened in 1965 was not so much a change as a return, was in fact *more* in keeping with American traditions than with what had gone on from the 1920s to 1965, is only exacerbated by Ludden's exclusion of that narrative in her reporting.

Even voices at the other end of the spectrum from Buchanan et al., those who see contemporary American immigration and diversity as unquestionable strengths, likewise tend to define them as strikingly new phenomena. On his website *Asian Nation*, UMass sociologist C.N. Le prominently features a piece on the 1965 Immigration Act, calling it "a significant watershed moment in Asian American history." Though of course Le is right that the Act did "reverse decades of systematic exclusion and restrictive immigration policies" and thus did allow for significantly greater Asian immigrations than had been possible for almost a century—and while a piece elsewhere on the site entitled "The First Asian Americans" does highlight the 19th century histories of Asian American immigration—his statements about the 1965 Act go further still: he says of its subsequent "new arrivals" that they "have transformed the demographic, economic, and cultural characteristics of many urban areas, the larger Asian American community, and mainstream American society in general." The last clause is the core of the narrative I'm tracing here. Some post-1965 transformations are indisputable: that many of the immigrants were newly legal after four or more decades of restriction; that they arrived from more distinct countries than ever before. But in the narrative I'm tracing here, as in Le's formulation, the post-1965 arrivals represented something far more sweeping: a shift in "mainstream American society," a radical break from what had constituted that society in any past era. Later in the article, Le calls these changes "a demographic revolution," and I would argue that such a phrase implies not in any sense a return to and amplification of past diversity, certainly not an extension of a longstanding, historical national community, but instead again a sea-change, a dramatic shift in America's defining identity.

In the same vein, journalist, activist, and self-identified illegal immigrant José Antonio Vargas (he was sent to the country by his parents when he was twelve, without authorization for a permanent stay, and, now over thirty, has recently "outed" himself) writes, in an inaugural piece for his "Define American" website and project, that "the immigration story is

DOI: 10.1057/9781137339096

a story about a demographically changing America," due to "the fourth wave of immigration that began in 1965, when the Immigration and Nationality Act... forever changed the ethnic make-up of our country." Vargas, like Le, wants to celebrate our contemporary diversity, indeed (as the project's name suggests) to make it central to how we define our nation and identity going forward. Yet he too, like each of these other distinct voices and yet similar narratives, sees that diversity as something fundamentally new, a late 20th and early 21st century shift in our history and community. And for the remainder of this chapter, I want to argue precisely the opposite: that America has been genuinely multicultural, uniquely and hugely diverse, since its origin points; that while the Chinese Exclusion Act and even more fully the 1920s laws did limit our immigration and thus our diversity in a variety of ways, it is they, not the 1965 Act, that represented a significant change; and that the 1965 Act and its aftermath thus constitute a return to and amplification of a defining American tradition and identity. Without question the demographics of America have changed since 1965 and are continuing to evolve in our contemporary moment[1]—but to see those changes as the next steps for an originating, ongoing, multiethnic American community and identity is quite distinct from seeing them as a shift away from what and where we've been.

Definitions of American identity as foundationally diverse and multiethnic have proliferated in academic scholarship over the past couple of decades, as I discovered while researching the book in which I offered my own such definition: *Redefining American Identity: From Cabeza de Vaca to Barack Obama* (2011). It's to better represent such images of America, after all, that so many American literature and history survey courses now begin not only with the Puritans and the English but also with Cabeza de Vaca and Bartolomé de las Casas, with the French and the Dutch, with Native American myths and speeches, and so on. Yet I would argue that in the broader community and classroom comprised by public conversations and debates, we scholars have largely failed to make the case for such visions of American identity; that instead, as the many figures I have just quoted illustrate, our national narratives of America's origins still emphasize a much more homogeneous starting point and frame diversity as a recent and ongoing shift (whether, again, a positive or negative one). And if we want to make the case instead for an originating and defining national diversity, one that was strikingly apparent by the late 19th century, was briefly curtailed in the early 20th century, and has returned with full force in the last few decades, the Chinese Exclusion Act provides a very effective starting point through which to develop those arguments.

* * *

Better remembering the Chinese Exclusion Act provides multiple arguments in favor of that longstanding American diversity. Asian Americans are often highlighted as a particularly new community within late 20th and early 21st century America: whether that point is connected to critiques of their presence (a la Buchanan's "never fully assimilated in any Western country") or celebrations of it (a la Le's *Asian Nation* site), this community has become the poster child for the 1965 Act's effects. Again, certainly the number of Asian nations and peoples involved has been amplified in the past few decades, particularly by refugee communities including Vietnamese, Cambodian, and Hmong Americans. Yet the simple fact is that there have been significant numbers of Asian Americans for nearly two hundred years, and likewise a multinational Asian American community for at least as long: the first Chinese immigrants appear on the 1820 census, by the early 1850s there were more than 25,000 Chinese Americans, and by the time of the Exclusion Act the population numbered well over 200,000; Japanese immigrants began to arrive in significant numbers in the 1870s, numbered in the thousands by 1880, and after the Exclusion Act became an even more sizeable immigrant population (nearly 25,000 were counted on the 1900 census), a trend that continued until the 1907–1908 "Gentleman's Agreement" that drastically restricted their arrivals; and Filipino immigrants represent perhaps the oldest Asian American community, having established a permanent settlement in southern Louisiana in the mid-18th century, fighting alongside other American troops under Jean Lafitte in the War of 1812's Battle of New Orleans, and founding the first U.S. Filipino Association in 1870, among other early historical landmarks. The histories and stories of each of these communities (among others) are hugely complex and demand individual engagement, but what they share is the basic and crucial fact of existence, across multiple centuries of American life.

Moreover, eliding or minimizing the long-term historical and cultural presences of these Asian American communities does more than just inaccurately reflect our national diversity: to my mind, it grants the Chinese Exclusion Act and its restrictive ilk precisely the discriminatory

DOI: 10.1057/9781137339096

and exclusive power for which they were created. By not only restricting future arrivals but also (among other changes) barring return trips and denying the possibility of citizenship to any already present Asian Americans—and even stripping such citizenship from some of those who had gained it, as I'll discuss in the next chapter—the Act and its follow up laws quite clearly sought to make life in the United States sufficiently difficult for these large, existing communities that they would shrink significantly. Whether they succeeded or not is beside the point (and to some small degree they did, although I believe most late 19th century Asian Americans did not leave the U.S.)—one of the most meaningful and productive ways to remember these Acts is precisely to recognize those destructive intentions, and even more to remember the large and longstanding American communities whose presence they challenged but couldn't erase. As I discussed in Chapter 1, the Know Nothing Party tried to oppose and restrict Irish immigration in the late 1840s and 1850s; they failed in their own era, but more importantly history has proven them entirely wrong, revealing the vital and ongoing contributions of Irish Americans in every aspect of our society and culture. Although the anti-Asian forces succeeded in passing legislation and forcing their xenophobic discrimination onto our national landscape, their long-term impact was no more justified, nor more lasting, than the Know Nothings'; the Asian American communities that long predated these laws have also long outlasted them and contributed far more to American society and culture. To forget those presences and their impacts (even as part of an argument in favor of the 1965 Immigration Act or contemporary diversity) would be as inaccurate to our history and identity as to treat Irish Americans as a recent community.

If we can successfully perform those two historical acts—recognizing the long-term presences of Asian American communities, and resisting the discriminatory effects of those laws that sought to exclude and erase such communities—we can and should extend them to other foundational, multicultural American communities. That's particularly relevant and important, I would argue, when it comes to the oldest European American community, Spanish (and subsequently Mexican) Americans. I think 21st century Americans do have a sense—thanks largely to the tourist industries in Florida and California—of just how far back the Spanish American community extends: Florida's St. Augustine, which was founded in 1565, is at least somewhat famous as the oldest continuously occupied European settlement in the United States; and similarly, the early missions and settlements at California cities such as San Diego (which was first explored right at the turn of the 17th century and fully founded by Father Juniper Serra about a century later) and the rest of the region known as Alta California (which likewise became fully settled in the mid-18th century) form a part of our histories of those places and regions. Obviously the same can be said for the U.S. Southwest in general, given the preponderance of Spanish names for and other Hispanic cultural presences within the region's states, cities, and communities. Yet it seems to me that our national narratives and definitions tend to treat these Spanish and Mexican communities as part of an alternative, past European trajectory for the Americas—as, that is, existing separate from and prior to, and thus entirely outside of, the subsequent "American" communities in these cities, states, and regions.

There are at least three interconnected ways to push back on those narratives and argue instead for these Spanish American communities as part of our originating national ones. For one thing, while it's true that they were settled and spent centuries under a different nation's (Spain's) flag, the simple fact is that the same can be said for every American region—I'll have more to say in a moment about the need to separate definitions of America from England, so for now will just note that the Puritan settlements in Massachusetts and the English colony in Virginia (for example) were no more politically or distinctly "American" at their founding and for the better part of two centuries afterward than were these Spanish settlements. Second, whatever flags flew over these settlements and during whatever periods, the truth is that many (if not most) of the Spanish and Mexican settlers remained in their communities after the legal handover to the United States and the arrival of Anglo settlers, making them not just a part of the area's history or geography but an ongoing and foundational presence in all these places. That continuity is reflected fully in a city like San Diego: the composition and community of Old Town, as the area first settled by Spanish arrivals has come to be known, did indeed change with the 1848 Treaty of Guadalupe Hidalgo, the Gold Rush, and the late 1840s and 1850s influx of Anglo settlers; but that change was much more fully one of addition than replacement, with Anglo homes, businesses, public officials, and the like complementing the existing and ongoing Mexican presences, leading to a city in which (as any visit to the area quickly reveals) the Spanish American histories and identities would continue to remain and evolve alongside these Anglo American ones.

DOI: 10.1057/9781137339096

The third way to push back on historical narratives of American identity that would exclude or separate Spanish and Mexican American communities is precisely to focus on the Treaty of Guadalupe Hidalgo and its aftermath. The Treaty is not in any sense the same as the Chinese Exclusion Act—not only because it originated as the peace treaty to conclude a war, but also (if relatedly) because it included provisions to protect Mexican communities living in the territories that were being transferred to the United States—but there's no question that it became nearly as discriminatory as the Exclusion Act: that in its aftermath, U.S. laws and legal responses consistently favored Anglo settlers (or, in many cases, squatters) over the rights and property of Mexican Americans. The result of this trend, as captured in late 19th century historical novels such as Helen Hunt Jackson's *Ramona* (1884) and María Amparo Ruiz de Burton's *The Squatter and the Don* (1885), was to dislocate many Mexican American families and communities, not only from their own lands but from American identity and history. Just as with the Chinese and other Asian American communities affected but not erased by the Exclusion Act, then, a vital part of remembering the history of Spanish and Mexican American communities lies in remembering such discriminatory laws and practices but not replicating, indeed resisting, their effects within our national narratives. Instead of performing our own erasures, that is, we can mirror what Mexican American activists have long called "El Retorno" (The Return): the recognition that 21st century Mexican Americans are quite literally the opposite of a new community, are instead returning to full presence in a land where they have been an originating and foundational culture.

Since many critiques of contemporary immigration or diversity hinge on fears about Mexican or Latino immigrants, often connected to narratives of the ways in which "these immigrants are different" from those who have come before, there are particularly significant stakes in recognizing such originating and foundational Spanish and Mexican American communities. Those anti-immigrant narratives are often likewise connected to the concept of "El Retorno," but reframed instead as "La Reconquista": the idea of a "Reconquest" of the Southwest that had been initially advanced by certain radical Latino writers and activists but has become in many cases a locus of xenophobic paranoia and hate. Yet such an idea, whether advanced as a positive goal or used as a demagogic source of fear and division, depends on histories in which Mexicans were

DOI: 10.1057/9781137339096

the subject of Anglo American conquest, were expelled and excluded by the arriving settlers and new government. And while certainly that process did take place far too often (particularly when compared to the guarantees contained in the Treaty), to my mind the broader and more meaningful reality is that Spanish and Mexican American communities were not solely or centrally defined by these discriminatory laws and responses, never left these places and cities, and have thus been a continuous and significant part of a post-contact America for as long as it has existed. As is true for Asian American communities, certainly the post-1965 era has seen an increase in the number and range of Latin American nationalities represented within American society; but once again, and even more fully for these Hispanic Americans, that increase is an amplification of a long-term, foundational national presence and community.

Moreover, working to better remember and incorporate Asian and Spanish American communities into our national histories can help us do the same for other too frequently elided communities, ones without quite as overtly negative or exclusionary experiences but with just as foundational and lasting presences on our American landscape. A good example would be the Dutch colony and settlers in New Netherland, including the capital city of New Amsterdam, a hugely significant colony and port in 17th century America. It's true that in the late 1660s and early 1670s the city and then the region were first surrendered (in the course of two of the period's multiple Anglo-Dutch wars) and later formally ceded to England (by the 1674 Treaty of Westminster), and were renamed New York thereafter. But it's also and even more significantly true that the Dutch settlers and communities remained in the region, becoming a complex and evolving part of colonial America, the Revolutionary era, and the new nation's identity beyond. As is often the case, the works of a prominent American literary and cultural figure, Washington Irving, can help us recognize and engage with this regional and national presence and history: Irving's *A History of New York, by Diedrich Knickerbocker* (1809) is partly a satire of early 19th century historians but also a multipart representation of this longstanding and continuing Dutch American community; and in short stories such as "Rip Van Winkle" (1819) Irving uses Knickerbocker's fictional researches into that community's stories and identities to create an American mythology, one set in "a little village of great antiquity, ... founded by some of the Dutch colonists," made up of "some of the houses of the original settlers," and constituting a present

DOI: 10.1057/9781137339096

and vibrant Dutch American community in the years immediately before and after the Revolution.

The same can and must be said about each of the regions and places acquired by the burgeoning American colonies, whether likewise during the colonial era or in the decades after the Revolution. That includes French settlements in the upper Midwest, such as at Detroit; the city had been founded by the French in 1701 and was surrendered to the English during the French and Indian War, but retained, as did much of Michigan and the region, significant aspects of its Franco-American presence, community, and culture. Likewise with the French, Spanish, and Creole communities on the Gulf Coast, and particularly in New Orleans; that city was founded by the French in 1718, transferred to Spain in the mid-18th century, returned to France in 1801, and then was sold to the United States as part of the 1803 Louisiana Purchase, but as the late 19th century historical writings of George Washington Cable (as well as any 21st century visit to the city) reflect, New Orleans has retained its multinational, multilingual, and multicultural community in the centuries since the Purchase. Similarly, the Russian settlers and communities in Alaska were in no significant way displaced or even particularly affected by the United States' post–Civil War purchase of the territory (colloquially known as Seward's Folly): those settlers, who had been in Alaska since at least the 1730s, remained in cities such as their capital of Sitka (known then as New Archangel) after the 1867 purchase; given the slow rate of further settlement (which didn't really pick up until the gold rushes of the late 19th and early 20th centuries), the territory remained largely Russian American (along with Native American) for many further decades, and the culture's presence and influence persist in numerous ways to this day.

I don't mean to suggest that there weren't significant changes in these communities after the transfers to English or U.S. ownership, or that the processes of transfer and new settlement weren't full of challenges, conflicts, and even violence. Yet despite those realities, I would say the same thing of all these places that I said of San Diego and its Old Town—that the changes much more frequently and significantly represented additions and new mixtures rather than replacements, with Anglo and other U.S. settlers and communities joining the existing cultural and national presences and creating new, multipart places and cultures. It's certainly true that the figures, institutions, and documents of government, of authority, of the place's official identity, did indeed change drastically

DOI: 10.1057/9781137339096

in each case, as illustrated most succinctly by the change in their governmental and formal language to English. Yet as George Washington Cable's historical novel of New Orleans after the Louisiana Purchase, *The Grandissimes* (1881), so thoroughly explores, these multinational and multicultural American cities and places, from New Orleans to Detroit, New York to San Diego, Sitka to Santa Fe, and many more, were and are defined by a multitude of language and voices, including but in no way limited to those of the governmental leaders and official texts.

Remembering that multilingual America existing beyond its official institutions and documents also represents one of two ways I would push back against an understandable but very limiting idea: that America's origin points lie in the Revolutionary era, and more specifically with the nation's founding political moments and documents. Certainly those documents, and the almost entirely Anglo American framers who drafted them, form a hugely significant part of the United States' political founding, one that has influenced the rest of the nation's history and identity in profound ways. Yet those documents and framers no more encompass the whole of American identity in 1776 (or at any other time) than, say, the post-Louisiana Purchase leadership and laws in New Orleans constituted the city's entire identity; or than the federal government of 2012 provides the sole means through which to define our contemporary community. Recognizing the framers' vital role is not at all the same as equating them or their documents with all of America's identity at that originating moment; and if we can separate a sense of their contributions from the idea that their particular identities and communities were any more foundational than the many other, contemporaneous such communities with which they were surrounded, we will have a much stronger sense of where America began.

Moreover, we don't even have to go outside of the thirteen original colonies in order to gain that sense. Certainly I believe that we should define an originating American identity as including the origins of every state and region that are now part of the nation; if Hawai'i is now an equal part of America to Massachusetts (and it unquestionably is), then its multicentury, multinational history and identity are just as equally all of ours as well. But as both the continuing Dutch American presence and community in New York and the mid-18th century influx of German immigrants to Pennsylvania against which Ben Franklin xenophobically protested illustrate, even the thirteen original colonies were far from solely or even centrally Anglo American in their composition. And there are multiple other transnational communities that would extend the point, including at least a couple that are almost always associated only with later waves of immigration: Jewish Americans in colonial and Revolutionary New England, a longstanding historical community about which my Fitchburg State University colleague Michael Hoberman has recently written in his *New Israel/New England: Jews and Puritans in Early America* (2011); and, even less familiar but perhaps even more significant to our national narratives, the late 18th century Moroccan Arab American community in South Carolina.

Not a great deal is known about the historical origins of that Moroccan community: many of its members might have descended from slaves (or even brought to the Americas as slaves themselves); others could have been immigrated, whether to escape contemporary dangers such as the region's Barbary Pirates or due to the encouragement of the 1786 Treaty of Friendship, signed by the United States and Morocco to protect U.S. shipping from those pirates and otherwise cement an international relationship between the two nations. Whatever their starting points, by 1790 their presence in South Carolina was prominent enough to occasion a bill in the state's legislature, the Moors Sundry Act: the law recognized the state's Moroccan residents (known at the time as "Moors") as "white," exempting them from laws governing free or enslaved African Americans and requiring certain other civic obligations of them (such as jury duty). Less overt, but to my mind clearly still connected, is a debate in the same legislature from two years earlier: as the state's legislators debated in 1788 whether to ratify the U.S. Constitution, the question was raised of whether that document's Article VI, paragraph 3, which states that "no religious test shall ever be required as a qualification to any office," would mean that a Muslim could successfully run for public office in the United States. One of the state's delegates to the Constitutional Convention, Charles Pinckney (who had contributed to drafting that paragraph), both argued that it did carry that meaning and expressed his hope that one day such an event would indeed come to pass. Whether or not Pinckney or any other legislator explicitly had the state's Moroccan American community in mind at this moment, the debate reflects that such multicultural diversity was a present and practical topic for Americans in the Revolutionary era, and both of these South Carolina decisions, complex as each was, likewise illustrate a nation already working to engage with and even strengthen that diversity in official and legal as well as social and communal ways.

DOI: 10.1057/9781137339096

America was thus already, I'm arguing, both significantly diverse and well able to incorporate and respond to that diversity by the Revolutionary era; by the time of the Chinese Exclusion Act, a hundred years later, it had diversified further still. This was a nation with significant and long-standing Asian American and Hispanic American communities; a country constituted of multinational, multicultural, and multilingual cities, states, and territories, and regions from coast to coast; a culture made up of a multilayered, cross-cultural combination of peoples and histories. America in 1882, that is, bore a striking resemblance to America in the late 20th and early 21st centuries; it was the Chinese Exclusion Act and the even more broadly exclusionary 1920s Immigration Acts that represented "a radical break" with "our national tradition," that sought by limiting our diversity to effect "profound demographic change." While the post-1965 era has indeed seen an increase in the number of nations and communities immigrating to and comprising America, that trend likewise mirrors the evolution of our nation from the first moments of contact through the early 20th century; the 1965 Act simply reversed the 1920s attempts to stop that trend, and the four decades of restrictive policies that followed them, returning us much more fully to our founding diversity and identity. It's certainly fair to note that for many older contemporary Americans, whose first years of life coincided with these most restrictive decades, "my country" might indeed feel much less diverse than 21st century America—but the overarching histories of American diversity tell a very different, and to my mind much more defining, story.

Taking this perspective on American diversity would drastically change our contemporary narratives and arguments, in multiple ways. For critics of diversity and multiculturalism like Buchanan, such concepts have been advanced post-1965, and are thus new and central influences in the dividing of our once-culturally-unified nation over the last half-century; but for that argument to hold any water, that cultural unity would have to have been actual, rather than mythic and constructed (or simply a partial effect of restrictive post-1920s immigration laws). On the other hand, for many supporters of diversity and multiculturalism, those qualities likewise relate to recent trends; although this perspective is more positive, it still envisions our diversity as something new, as a fundamental change from what we had been, and thus both unintentionally reinforces the goals of those exclusionary immigration laws and, frankly, makes possible arguments like Buchanan's about these "changes"

DOI: 10.1057/9781137339096

to "our national tradition." Whereas if we understand that the diversity is what has always defined and unified us, that our nation and community have been built out of multiple cultures and nations, multiple peoples and histories and voices and languages, from their origin points, then we can push past the myths, and past the divisions too, and recognize the multicultural America that we have all shared. Helping us recognize such a genuinely shared and unifying national identity is a powerful purpose for which public scholars can and should work. And we can do so with great success by starting with what the Chinese Exclusion Act can teach us about diversity.

Note

1 As illustrated by the prominent May 2012 news stories about "minority" births out-numbering "white" ones for the first time.

DOI: 10.1057/9781137339096

3

What the Act Can Teach Us about Forgotten and Inspiring American Stories

Abstract: *Better remembering the Chinese Exclusion Act would also help us connect to potent examples of what has always been most right about America, in the form of profoundly inspiring American identities and stories: those of the poets who carved their texts on the walls of Angel Island's holding facility; those of Yung Wing, his evolving Chinese American life and identity, and his multigenerational American family; and those of Yung's 120 students at the Chinese Educational Mission, their own Chinese American experiences and lifelong impacts, and their climactic victory on an Oakland baseball field.*

Keywords: Angel Island; baseball in America; Chinese Americans; Chinese Educational Mission; Chinese Exclusion Act; Yung Wing

Railton, Ben. *The Chinese Exclusion Act: What It Can Teach Us about America.* New York: Palgrave Macmillan, 2013. DOI: 10.1057/9781137339096.

The walls of Angel Island contain a far too little known, profoundly inspiring treasure trove of American voices and writing. In 1910, twenty-eight years after the passage of the Chinese Exclusion Act and at the height of Asian exclusion (with Japanese and other Asian immigrants now similarly limited and excluded by subsequent laws and extensions), Angel Island in San Francisco Bay was opened as a West Coast national immigration station. Although its function ostensibly paralleled that of Ellis Island, Angel Island's true purpose was less to facilitate the arrival and processing of new immigrants and more to detain (and usually deport) all those whose immigration was banned by the exclusionary laws (which was the vast majority of those who arrived on the West Coast). As such, Angel Island included an extensive holding center—or prison—in which thousands of largely Chinese and some other Asian immigrants were detained for weeks and months (and in some cases years), bunked in 100-person communal rooms, uncertain of whether they would ever be allowed to enter the United States (or re-enter, since many prior residents and even citizens were also excluded by the Act) or of when their situation would change in any way.

By the time Angel Island closed its doors thirty years later, in 1940, nearly 200,000 arrivals had been detained there, and a significant number of them had very literally made their mark on the site: writing poems (mostly in Chinese, a few in English) on the building's walls. Many of those poems have been saved and translated—Angel Island and most of its buildings have been preserved as part of a California State Park, and scholars Him Mark Lai, Genny Lim, and Judy Yung have edited an excellent anthology and textbook entitled *Island Poetry and History of Chinese Immigrants on Angel Island, 1910–1940*—and they represent a truly unique, diverse, and compelling community of American texts and voices: an archive that is as literary as it is historical, as individual as it is communal, as thoughtful as it is emotional, as inspiring as it is tragic. As one of the poems begins, capturing both the poems' central emotional tones and their ability to serve as collective memory, "There are tens of thousands of poems on these walls / They are all cries of suffering and sadness / The day I am rid of this prison and become successful / I must remember that this chapter once existed." And others examine additional, equally complex elements of the community's experiences and situation: "With a gentle breeze I arrived at the city thinking it would all be so / At ease, how was one to know he was to live in a wooden building?"; "America has power, but not justice / In prison, we were victimized as if we were guilty / Given no opportunity to explain, it was really brutal"; "This is a message to those who live here not to worry excessively / Instead, you must cast your idle worries to the flowing stream / Experiencing a little ordeal is not hardship / Napoleon was once a prisoner on an island."

As that last poem indicates, the Angel Island poems served explicitly present and practical (as well as literary and philosophical) purposes, allowing the poets not only to express their own perspectives but also to communicate with each other and their fellow detainees, across the years and the many generations that experienced the Exclusion Act's effects. Similarly, the main arguments I would make for a fuller national awareness of and engagement with the poems include on the one hand the value of hearing those individual perspectives, of making sure that these talented and interesting American writers gain the place in our literary and national history that they unquestionably deserve; and on the other hand the need to do full justice to their cross-generational goals, to allow them to speak to our own contemporary moment and community. The issues of immigration history and diversity about which I've written in my first two chapters, after all, can seem overly broad or general without human faces and voices to which to connect them, and the Angel Island poems provide some of our most unique and compelling such human connections for those issues and many others.

I would also highlight a third, slightly different, equally vital benefit to better remembering the poems, however. More full and accurate public knowledge of the histories of American immigration law and diversity, the goal for which I've worked in my first two chapters, is without doubt a worthwhile pursuit; but that knowledge often focuses, as did many of my specifics in those chapters, on more dark and destructive parts of our national history and identity. From the Chinese Exclusion Act to the 1920s quota-producing laws, the illegal expulsion of Mexican American homeowners from their property to the elision of numerous other communities from our national narratives, many of the histories that we have so thoroughly forgotten are grounded in discrimination and prejudice, in legal and social (and often also genuine) violence against multiple American peoples and communities. Obviously I believe that there's great value in remembering those histories, but there's certainly also potential limitation, since it's all too easy for our memories of them to reinforce and even amplify the kinds of cultural divisions and hostilities on which they often focus. At the very least, it can be difficult to imagine creating unifying and even inspiring national identities and communities

DOI: 10.1057/9781137339096

through awareness of our most divided and dark pasts. And to my mind, it's vitally important that American scholars, like all Americans, maintain the possibility of being inspired about and by America, not in a simplistic or jingoistic way but through a genuine, shared recognition of some of the best of what we've been and can be. Otherwise, we risk becoming the caricatured, one-note anti-American radicals that the most stereotyping public narratives imagine us to be, and likely losing in the process any chance to have an impact on American audiences and conversations in corrective *and* inspiring ways.

So how do we more fully and accurately remember the histories of immigration and diversity, along with the specific and far-too-often divisive and destructive elements and moments within those histories (such as the Chinese Exclusion Act), yet find ways to be unified and inspired at the same time? By likewise better remembering the kinds of genuinely powerful American identities and voices, stories and histories that parallel, exist alongside of, and even come directly out of those darkest moments and histories. The Angel Island poets and their poems represent one amazing community of such voices and stories, one that certainly reveals the darkest depths of the Exclusion Act's effects and era yet that also exemplifies the kinds of inspiring strength, perseverance, and individual and communal power that Americans have so often found in the face of such dark moments. Since those poets and poems, like too many inspiring American voices and texts, are not familiar to most Americans, bringing them to our collective attention depends precisely on the work of public scholars. And fuller national awareness of and engagement with the Chinese Exclusion Act can likewise connect us very directly to two other, interconnected and inspiring American stories and histories, two collections of identities and moments that similarly aren't at all present in our dominant national narratives, when to my mind they should be at the heart of them.

* * *

Ironically, the man at the center of both inspiring stories, Chinese American diplomat, soldier, and educator Yung Wing, was in the 19th century without question one of the most famous Asian Americans.[1] Each significant stage of Yung's transnational life and journey received coverage in the *New York Times*, for example, with his marriage and death (both of which I'll discuss more below) garnering the kind of

DOI: 10.1057/9781137339096

attention reserved for prominent public figures. Yet despite that contemporary prominence, and notwithstanding the fact that an elementary school (P.S. 124) in New York City's Chinatown is named after Yung, I believe that few Americans—and in my experience none outside of the academic historical and Chinese American communities—have heard of Yung at all, and that even fewer know any of the details of his complex, conflicted, impressive, and profoundly inspiring life.[2] Fortunately for those of us who want to share those details, in his final years of life Yung published a memoir, *My Life in China and America* (1909)[3], that provides an excellent starting point for analyzing some of his most complex and crucial American moments.

The fact that Yung was able to publish his memoir, like the amount of newspaper coverage his life received, does reflect an element of his identity that I should foreground from the outset: his privileged status, at least compared to nearly all of his fellow 19th century Asian immigrants (who began arriving in significant numbers at exactly the same moment of Yung's initial immigration, the late 1840s). They traveled to the west coast of America on dangerously crowded and unsafe voyages, to perform difficult labor (constructing railroad lines, for example) and faced a variety of discriminations aimed at all "coolies" (the era's standard derogatory term for Asian laborers); Yung journeyed to the east coast with two peers and a pair of Anglo missionaries, to attend Christian preparatory school and then college as an exemplary representative of his homeland. In discussing Yung's identity and experiences at length, I don't want to replicate that final assumption, to treat him as necessarily representative of all (or indeed any) 19th century Chinese or Asian Americans; the more we can learn about the variety of identities and experiences comprised by those communities, the richer and stronger our national histories will become. But on the other hand, just as Yung's relatively privileged status did not in any way exempt him from the effects of the Chinese Exclusion Act and its aftermath, neither should the more singular nature of his experiences elide their impressive and inspiring details and meanings.

Moreover, one of the most impressive aspects of Yung's identity, both as he frames it in the memoir and as he lived it across his multiple stages and settings, was his desire to work for the three distinct communities to which he was connected: China, the United States, and the burgeoning Chinese American population. Three very different turning points, and the sections of the memoir in which Yung addresses them, reflect

DOI: 10.1057/9781137339096

these efforts with particularly clarity. The first came very early in Yung's American experiences—in 1850, having spent two years at Monson (Massachusetts) Academy, Yung was faced with a difficult choice: to return to China, as his two fellow students did (one immediately, the other after completing his medical education in Scotland) or to find a way to attend Yale, and more exactly (since Yung admits that this option was his clear preference) to find a way to pay for that further education. As Yung writes in the opening of Chapter V, "My College Days," some trustees of the academy pledged to support his college education if he would promise to return to China as a missionary immediately after graduation; but Yung declined, recognizing that "the calling of a missionary is not the only sphere in life where one can do the most good in China or elsewhere," and that in the future he "might be obliged to create new conditions, if I found old ones were not favorable to any plan I might have" (13). As he contemplated the goals of that college education—for which he did find alternative funding, becoming the first Chinese student to attend and graduate from Yale—he began to develop precisely such a new plan, one that would help "the rising generation of China enjoy the same educational advantages that I had enjoyed," the same connections to "western education" and to America through it (15). That plan, which Yung would come to call the "Chinese Educational Mission" and for which he would work steadily for the next three decades, thus represented his goal of "grafting Western education to the Oriental culture, a union destined to weld together the different races of the world into one brotherhood" (27).

After his 1854 graduation from Yale, Yung spent much of the next two decades traveling and in China, pursuing various professional, diplomatic, and military projects while continuously "weaving the educational scheme"; it was in the course of those travels that he experienced the second and third significant turning points in his evolving Chinese American identity. In the spring of 1864, Yung returned to the United States; his official purpose was to purchase machinery for the Chinese military, in which he had been given a "civil rank." Unofficially, Yung hoped that the return represented a "preliminary step that would ultimately lead to the realization of my educational scheme, which had never for a moment escaped my mind." But while in America, Yung took instead another surprising and deeply inspiring step: meeting with "the general in charge of the [Union Army's] Volunteer Department," Yung expressed his feeling that, "as a naturalized citizen of the United States, it

DOI: 10.1057/9781137339096

was my bounden duty to" enlist in the army, "simply to show my loyalty and patriotism to my adopted country." In his memoir Yung downplays the moment's significance, noting that "it would take at least six months before the" machinery order could be filled, and so he was simply "offering my services to the government in the meantime"; the general apparently responded in kind, thanking Yung but arguing that "since you are charged with a responsible trust to execute for the Chinese government, you had better return... to attend to it. We have plenty of men to serve." Yet neither Yung's humility nor the general's "preemptory decision" (the rationale for which we can never know) should mask this moment's singular courage and impressiveness: at one of America's most divided and fragile moments, in a war when many wealthy Northerners bought their way out of military service, and during a period of that war when General Grant's aggressive tactics were producing ever higher numbers of casualties (on both sides), this immigrant American, a man who had been able to spend only six of the prior sixteen years in the United States, volunteered to serve his new home (54–55).

Yung's third turning point took place almost a decade later, in 1873, and reflected yet another side to his service to China, America, and the growing transnational community in between. By this time his educational mission had already come to fruition, as I will discuss momentarily, but Yung likewise continued to travel to China for various diplomatic and military purposes. On one such journey to the city of Tientsin, he met with the Peruvian commissioner, who was there "to make a treaty with China regarding the further importation of coolie labor into Peru"; the commissioner "pictured to [Yung] in rosy colors how well the Chinese were treated in Peru," but Yung, relying on his own knowledge "of the facts and horrors of the coolie traffic," proffered no support for "this diabolical business" and instead offered the Chinese viceroy his service in "looking into the condition of the Chinese coolies" in Peru. His offer accepted, Yung spent three months in Peru (while at his urging a peer, Chin Lan Pin, was doing the same in Cuba, the era's other most prominent site of the traffic), collecting information and taking "two dozen photographs" for a thorough report that "would tell a tale of cruelty and inhumanity... which would be beyond cavil and dispute." Indeed, the report and accompanying "photographs proved to be so incontrovertible and palpable" that the proposed treaty was withdrawn and, Yung writes, "the traffic had received its death blow" (67–68). There are, to be sure, significantly more complex contexts, histories, and details to these

DOI: 10.1057/9781137339096

issues and changes than Yung can or does address in his memoir (or could engage with in his life), but nonetheless the report represents an additional layer of Yung's inspiring efforts to forge a stronger, healthier, and more genuinely connected Chinese American (in the broadest, hemispheric sense) community.

By far the most long-term of those efforts, of course, was the Chinese Educational Mission (CEM), and by the early 1870s Yung had finally reached a moment when he could propose it fully and successfully to the Chinese and American governments: an opportunity to educate 120 young Chinese men at select schools (secondary, preparatory, and college) throughout New England, for up to fifteen years each; a chance for them to continue their development both as Chinese citizens ("Chinese teachers were to be provided to keep up their knowledge of Chinese while in the United States") and as Chinese Americans ("all candidates were required...to begin the study of English or to continue with their English studies"). Although he packaged it along with three other proposals for the continued development of China, both internally and in the international community, it was the Educational Mission "in which [Yung's] whole heart was enlisted" (60). And among the many salient details of the Mission as Yung designed it, and perhaps the most meaningful, was his plan to build a "permanent headquarters in the United States" (in Hartford, Connecticut), so as to have "the educational mission as deeply rooted in the United States as possible" (66). To my mind, it was to that same end that Yung negotiated, as part of the Mission's existence and under the auspices of the 1868 Burlingame Treaty, the opportunity for advanced students "to make application to the State Department for admittance to the Military Academy at West Point and the Naval Academy in Annapolis" (72). That is, while Yung framed the military training as part of the students' preparation for service in China (and while I'm sure that was a genuine goal), the overarching point is that Yung designed the students' experiences to mirror quite precisely his own background and ideals: multipart American educational experiences over many years, an abiding connection to both China and America, an opportunity for military service in their new home, a chance to put down their own deep roots across the different communities that would comprise their evolving identities.

It's far from coincidental that in these same years Yung was likewise becoming significantly more rooted in Connecticut, the United States, and his own evolving Chinese American identity. In March of 1875,

DOI: 10.1057/9781137339096

Yung married Mary Kellogg of Avon, Connecticut; he doesn't write at all about the marriage in his memoir (perhaps out of a sense of privacy), but a March 2nd *New York Times* notice entitled "Yung Wing Marries a Connecticut Lady" documented the event. Three interconnected details particularly stand out in that brief notice: that Mary "wore a dress of white crape, imported expressly for this occasion from China"; that "the groom, who long since adopted our style, appeared in full evening dress"; and that at the reception "Chinese delicacies were mingled with...dishes of American style." Clearly the ceremony was as complicatedly and inspiringly Chinese American as the couple being wed—and when Yung writes later in his memoir about his and Mary's two sons, Morrison Brown Yung and Bartlett Golden Yung, he emphasizes precisely that complex hybridity: noting first that "they are most faithful, thoughtful and affectionate sons, and I am proud of their manly and earnest Christian characters" (77); praising their adoptions into "the best families in New England" and his elder son's subsequent admission to Yale after (as I will discuss) Yung was forced to leave America (79); and yet later highlighting their travels and efforts with him on Chinese diplomatic missions, part of their "devotion" to their father and his own transnational heritage and roles. In his life with Mary, and most clearly in this next generation of the Kellogg and Yung families, we can see just how fully Yung had achieved the communal and individual experience that he hoped the Mission would help create.[4]

Tragically, those dual achievements—in Yung's own life and with the Mission—would last less than a decade before the rising tide of anti-Chinese sentiment would sweep them both away. In his memoir's long and crucial Chapter XIX, "End of the Educational Mission," Yung focuses at first on changes in the Chinese government, the rise to power of certain traditionalist figures who distrusted Yung, the United States, and as a result efforts like the Mission's. While I do not believe that these figures could have shut down the Mission in the absence of the American anti-Chinese fervor, their disagreements with Yung reflect quite directly his own transnational, evolving Chinese American perspective and goals: with his central such traditionalist adversaries, minister Chin Lan Pin and commissioner Woo Tsze Tung, Yung debated precisely how much exposure to America the students should have, "standing as a kind of buffer" between the traditionalists and the students and advocating for the students' "change of costume, their attendance at Sunday School and church services, their outdoor exercises and athletic games," and most

DOI: 10.1057/9781137339096

of all for the benefits of "the gradual but marked transformation of the students in their behavior and conduct as they grew in knowledge and stature under New England influence" (70).[5] Although these disagreements unfortunately helped set the stage for the end of the Mission, at the same time they make clear just how fully the Mission was succeeding at creating the kinds of identities and community for which Yung had so consistently hoped and worked. "Now in New England the heavy weight of repression and suppression was lifted from the minds of these young students," Yung writes; "they exulted in their freedom and leaped for joy" (70).

While the core of those effects, I will argue, could not be destroyed, not by traditionalist opponents nor by American bigots, there's no question that 1878 saw a return of repression and suppression to the lives of the Mission's students. It was in that year that Yung deemed some of the first crop of students "advanced enough in their studies" for him to apply for their admission to the military academies, as supported by the Burlingame Treaty and outlined in the Mission's founding proposal. The rest of Yung's paragraph on this moment is worth quoting at length:

> The answer to my application was: "There is no room provided for Chinese students." It was curt and disdainful. It breathed the spirit of Kearnyism and Sandlotism[6] with which the whole Pacific atmosphere was impregnated, and which had hypnotized all the departments of the government, especially Congress, in which Blaine figured most conspicuously as the champion against the Chinese on the floor of the Senate.... The race prejudice against the Chinese was so rampant and rank that not only my application for the students to gain entrance to Annapolis and West Point was treated with cold indifference and scornful hauteur, but the Burlingame Treaty of 1868 was, without the least provocation, and contrary to all diplomatic precedents and common decency, trampled under foot unceremoniously and wantonly, and set aside as though no such treaty had ever existed, in order to make way for those acts of congressional discrimination against Chinese immigration which were pressed for immediate enactment. (72)

Yung's culminating connection, of this 1878 moment to the 1882 Chinese Exclusion Act, represents a particularly significant argument. After all, it was officially the Chinese government's decision to close the Mission and recall all 120 students; both efforts were completed by 1881, and so while they took place in response to the explicit affront and treaty violation of the military academy refusal, they did not explicitly fall under the parameters of the Exclusion Act. Partly Yung refers here to an 1880

DOI: 10.1057/9781137339096

revision of the Burlingame Treaty, a change that allowed the U.S. government to suspend Chinese immigration (although it did not actually do so until the Exclusion Act two years later). But more than that, Yung is contextualizing every aspect of the Mission's closing in the most salient contemporary history: the rising trend of anti-Chinese nativism and bigotry that had by this time reached every level of the government (the Treaty was revised at the order of President Hayes) and outside of which no Chinese American life or community could exist. The Chinese traditionalists might have wanted to close the Mission in any case, that is, but it took the American xenophobia and discriminatory laws to uproot the Mission and its powerful, evolving American connections.

That uprooting was only the first of three painful upheavals in Yung's life, "blows that fell upon me one after the other... [and] were enough to crush my spirit" (77). In the two years after the Mission's closure, Yung was recalled to China and sent on various diplomatic duties, and by the time he returned home in 1883, he found his wife gravely ill, both in body and in spirit; she had been told by a recently returned missionary that Yung was likely to have his head cut off in China "on account of the Chinese Educational Mission," and "this piece of gratuitous information tended more to aggravate a mind already weighed down by poor health" and "gloomy foreboding" (76). For the next three years the family would travel to various American places in an effort to find better climate for her recuperation, but in June 1886, only eleven years after her marriage to Yung, and with their sons only nine and seven years old, Mary died. "Her death made a great void in my after-life, which was irreparable," Yung admits—willing, perhaps even compelled, to write about this darkest moment with the kinds of private and emotional details that he had not shared of their courtship or marriage—"but she did not leave me hopefully deserted and alone; she left me two sons who are constant reminders of her beautiful life and character." For the next decade, Yung, with the help of his mother-in-law (also named Mary Kellogg), served as "both father and mother" to Morrison and Bartlett, his "whole soul wrapped up in their education and well-being" (77)—a period in his life that is perhaps the most inspiring of all, and that certainly symbolizes how fully his own Chinese American identity and experiences were intertwined with those of his boys.

Yet the discriminatory effects of the Chinese Exclusion Act would threaten even that familial relationship. In 1896, Yung was once again recalled to China, this time to deal with the aftermath of the Sino-Japanese

DOI: 10.1057/9781137339096

war (and subsequently with the coup of 1898); it was at this time that he took great pains to make sure his sons were sent to live with prominent New England families, and plans made for their continuing educations and futures. Despite those new living arrangements, Yung had no reason to think that this return to China represented a genuine break from his familial or American connections—but in April 1898 Yung's status as a naturalized American citizen was revoked, making it impossible for him to re-enter the United States legally. The brief letter in which Secretary of State John Sherman relayed this decision (to Charles Denby, a diplomat who had been corresponding with Yung) contains one of the most blunt and revealing paragraphs in any American text:

> Inasmuch as Yung Wing appears to have been granted his certificate of naturalization, a refusal to admit now his right to privileges which he has apparently exercised for many years would on its face seem unjust and without warrant. Nevertheless, in view of the construction placed upon the naturalization laws of the United States by our highest courts, the Department does not feel that it can properly recognize him as a citizen of the United States.[7]

With that, Yung's half-century of American experiences were cast aside, and he became nothing more than a potential illegal immigrant to the country to which he had become so thoroughly connected and had given so much over those decades. In his memoir, he mentions only one further return to the United States, a special 1902 visit to see Bartlett graduate from Yale; the government allowed Yung to enter for the occasion, and, as the *New York Times* reported, "among the guests of the university who had seats upon the platform during the exercises were Dr. Yung Wing of Hartford, Conn., a graduate of Yale and formerly minister from China to the United States."

By law, Yung could not remain in the United States after that occasion (unless he was on a diplomatic mission from China, which he wasn't). Yet I believe that he did, and that in fact he spent at least a portion of the rest of his decade of life in America. For one thing, Yung ends his memoir in 1902, despite it being published in 1909; perhaps the publication process took seven years, but perhaps Yung had spent some of those years doing something he would not necessarily wish to document: living illegally in the United States. And we have at least one strong piece of textual evidence that he did just that: his April 22, 1912 *New York Times* obituary, which was submitted to the paper from Hartford and which notes that

Yung "died at his home here today, in his eighty-fourth year." The piece goes on to focus on his different experiences and roles, both in China and within the United States; in the final paragraph, the writer adds simply that "in 1902 he came back to America." Again, that does not mean that Yung necessarily stayed after 1902, and legally he could not have; but I nonetheless hope and believe that he did so as much as he was able, for the sake of the home and life he had created here, and for the sake of the two men mentioned in the obituary's last sentence: "He leaves two sons, Morrison, of Hartford, and Bartlett, who is now at Shanghai." As those two locations reflect, Yung's sons had indeed carried forward his transnational Chinese American life and identity; I can think of no more inspiring final stage to that life than one in which Yung continued to make America part of it and part of his home, despite—indeed, in direct contrast to—the xenophobic laws that sought to exclude him from it and it from him.

If Yung's sons most definitely embodied and carried forward that Chinese American identity for which he had so consistently worked, so too, in their own ways, did the students of the Chinese Educational Mission, whose stories and identities represent the final inspiring American history I wish to highlight briefly in this chapter. Each of their individual stories and identities is of course both unique and extremely interesting, and I can't possibly do justice to them here; the *Chinese Educational Mission Connections* website (www.cemconnections.org) has begun to collect extensive biographical information on all 120 students, and their evolving database represents a powerful resource for all further exploration into this group of inspiring Chinese American lives. The website's information focuses on experiences both during and after their time in the United States, and thus provides glimpses into not only the Mission's era and its students' experiences but also the many ways in which they carried those American experiences forward into their subsequent, evolving lives and identities. Even though all 120 students were ostensibly sent back to China with the Mission's 1881 closure, many maintained explicit connections with and returned to the United States over subsequent years (or even found ways not to leave at all); and even those who didn't were, as I believe their biographical details reflect, greatly influenced by their transnational education, experiences, and communities.[8]

Two very distinct student biographies can provide a bit more detail on these ideas. Chang Hon Yen represents one of the students who worked

DOI: 10.1057/9781137339096

hard to remain in and connected to the United States and its Chinese American community: a graduate of Yale and then Columbia Law School, Chang was initially refused admission to the New York bar, but with the aid of a local judge fought for and then wrote himself a special bill through which the New York legislature granted him an exception and allowed him to pass the bar. He subsequently traveled to San Francisco and worked on behalf of the Chinese American community there, both those already in the United States and those seeking access (those, that is, held at Angel Island); he continued in that role for years (while working as a banker in the city) despite being denied legal standing by the California Supreme Court on account of being a "Mongolian." In subsequent years he would advise the Chinese Consulate in San Francisco, become himself the Chinese Consul to Vancouver, serve for a time as the First Secretary of the Chinese Legation in Washington, D.C., and direct Chinese naval students in Berkeley, among numerous other roles. By all accounts Chang simply refused to allow the Exclusion Act and its discriminatory effects and corollaries to derail his evolving Chinese American life and work, and clearly each nation, and many communities within both, were profoundly impacted as a result.

Jeme Tien Yau, on the other hand, reflects those students who returned to China after the Mission's closure but who nonetheless carried forward their education and experiences in a variety of inspiring ways. After attending high school in New Haven (and playing on the Mission's baseball team, on which more in a moment), Jeme attended Yale, graduating in 1881 with a degree in civil engineering. He returned to China for good in 1881, but continued that education and career very fully, first at the Fuzhou Naval School (through which he conducted the first Chinese survey of the Guangdong coastline) and then as the Chief Engineer for numerous railway lines and projects across China. In 1910 he received his doctorate in Engineering, and six years later became the first Chinese student to receive an honorary LL.D. (a doctorate in law) from Hong Kong University. He served for many years as a member and officer with the Chinese Institute of Engineers, the American Society of Civil Engineers, and the Institute of Civil Engineers of Britain. And in 1908, his two sons traveled to the United States as part of a special embassy and remained to enter college, one to study mechanical engineering at New York's Tri-State College and the other civil engineering at Yale. In both his son's lives and his own impressive and inspiring life and career, Jeme exemplifies how much every one of the Mission students carried

DOI: 10.1057/9781137339096

forward Yung's goals and hopes, whether in China, in America, or, most frequently, in a complex transnational combination of both worlds and communities.

Even at their collective low point, the immediate aftermath of the Mission's closure, the students experienced, and in fact created, one more deeply inspiring American moment and story, with which I want to close this chapter. During their time in New England, some of the students had formed a baseball team, known officially as the Orientals but usually referred to as the Celestials. William Lyon Phelps, a high school and college classmate of many of the students and later a prominent literary scholar at Yale, would write a chapter of his *Autobiography* (1939) on his "Chinese Schoolmates," and focused a good deal there on their athletic successes in a variety of sports and endeavors; he highlights in particular their baseball talents, and notes that one of the Celestials' pitchers, "Tsang [probably Wu Yangzeng],...was a great pitcher, impossible to hit." I have seen some secondary sources that indicate that another of the team's star pitchers, most likely Liang Dunyan, was nicknamed Lefty; while I haven't been able to confirm that detail in any of the era's primary sources, it would certainly add one more layer to the American mythos of the team, and reflects in any case the kinds of new identities to which the Mission was connecting these students (and which Yung defended so vigorously from his traditionalist colleagues' critiques). And whatever their nicknames, Wu, Liang, and their fellow players had considerable success on the local baseball circuit, and by the time of the Mission's closure had developed a reputation as a talented team.

With that closure, most of the students traveled to San Francisco, to await a steamer back to China. While they were waiting for that departure from their new homeland, a local Oakland baseball team challenged the Celestials to a game; it's impossible to know whether the challenge represented good sportsmanship or another side to the state's and nation's rising anti-Chinese fervor, whether it was an attempt to rise above the Kearnyism or an opportunity to provide an athletic counterpart to such bigotry. In either case, at least according to fellow student Wen Bing Chung, "the Oakland men imagined that they were going to have a walk-over with the Chinese."[9] But Lefty had his good stuff, the team rose to this almost impossibly difficult to imagine occasion, and the Celestials won their final game—and then boarded their steamer to carry them away from America.[10]

DOI: 10.1057/9781137339096

It's easy, as I noted at the outset of this chapter, to focus on the kinds of histories symbolized by that last detail: on the Chinese Exclusion Act, on its xenophobic contexts and causes and its painful and divisive effects, and so on the kinds of destructive American histories to which the Act unquestionably connects. If public scholars are going to work to teach Americans about the histories of immigration and diversity, to bring more complex and accurate versions of those national stories into our communal conversations, then a significant part of that work is indeed going to entail forcing us to confront more fully these darkest sides to our past and identity. And moreover, on the most human and perhaps most compelling level, we certainly can't tell the stories of the Chinese Educational Mission students, nor of Yung Wing, nor of the Angel Island poets, without including the Act and those darker histories very fully.

But why should the Act be any more central to those Americans' stories and histories than their acts?: the poets' expressions on the Angel Island walls; Yung's volunteering for the Union Army and his multidecade efforts to stay connected to his American home and family and sons; the students' individual lives and transnational impacts; the Celestials' triumphant final victory in that most American of sports. Each of those acts, and each of the many more that comprised these Chinese American lives and stories, identities, and communities, offers an inspiring glimpse into the best of America, into what our national ideals and narratives can mean when enacted, embodied, and exemplified by Americans struggling with, responding to, and most definitely transcending the darker and more divided national histories. I can't imagine anything more significant, and more unifying, than remembering and celebrating such Americans. I can't think of more meaningful work for public scholars than helping us do so. And I don't know of any history that can better connect us to and teach us about such Americans than that of the Chinese Exclusion Act.

Notes

1 Because the order of first and last names is generally reversed in Chinese (as compared to English), I will refer to Yung Wing in subsequent references as Yung. The other best candidate for the century's most famous Chinese American would likely be Wong Chin Foo; for more on Wong see Scott Seligman's biography (slated for a June 2013 release), which calls Wong in its title *The First Chinese American*.

DOI: 10.1057/9781137339096

2 This is only anecdotal evidence, but my sons' Chinese American grandparents, who immigrated to the United States in the 1960s and for the past three decades have lived in Connecticut (where Yung likewise spent nearly all of his time in America), knew Yung's name and that he had graduated from Yale but no other details of his American experiences or identity.

3 The full text of Yung's memoir, along with many other relevant historical documents and materials, is available online (in addition to the published versions held by various libraries and collections) at the wonderful Yung Wing Project, http://ywproject.x10.mx/.

4 To be clear, I'm not arguing that Yung necessarily intended for the CEM students to marry in America and create multicultural and -generational Chinese American families. Rather, I believe that the CEM plan, from its earliest origins to every aspect of its design and execution, represented Yung's attempt to bring together China and America and create new communities and identities out of that intersection, ones that would no matter their specifics thus parallel Yung's own evolving life and experiences.

5 These debates and different perspectives, as well as many of the details of the students and their experiences to which I will refer below, are collected and presented at the excellent *Chinese Educational Mission Connections* website (http://www.cemconnections.org/).

6 Kearnyism refers to Denis Kearney, the San Francisco-area labor leader and inveterate anti-Chinese racist who contributed greatly to the nation's rising nativist sentiment and the ultimate passage of the Exclusion Act. Since Kearney and his peers often addressed crowds in San Francisco's sandlots, their movement was also known as Sandlotism.

7 Sherman refers to the court cases I discussed in Chapter 1, those that upheld the Exclusion Act and its subsequent extensions. The full text of this letter is transcribed at the *Yung Wing Project* website.

8 Just as I did with Yung, I should make clear that I don't intend to treat the Mission students as representative of all Chinese Americans in this era. For the vast majority of Chinese (and Asian) immigrants, as I discussed above, their experiences of and with America were significantly different from those of the students, and deserve their own attention and remembrance. But nonetheless, the students' experiences and identities form another, and to my mind a powerful and inspiring, Chinese American community, and one we can and should include in our national histories. Again, given the CEM's ostensible emphasis on enhancing the students' service to China, my description of them as Chinese American is certainly debatable—but I believe both that it was Yung's goal to create such transnational identities, mirroring and carrying forward his own, and that the students' resulting experiences prove that he succeeded in doing so.

DOI: 10.1057/9781137339096

9 This quote, and other details of the team and this game, can be found in Joel S. Franks' contribution to the book *The American Game: Baseball and Ethnicity* (2002).

10 The pitcher in this final game was not specifically identified in Wen's account; but Wen does note that the pitcher was a Yale man, which was the case with Liang (and not with Wu, the team's other best pitcher). Per a 9/4/1881 story in the *San Francisco Chronicle*, the Celestials won the game 11–8. I am indebted to an anonymous reviewer for supplementing my own knowledge of many of these details.

DOI: 10.1057/9781137339096

Conclusion: So What?

Abstract: *Better remembering the Chinese Exclusion Act does not only teach us lessons about American history, culture, and identity, it also connects to and influences contemporary issues and debates. Those include the Obama administration's deportation policies toward illegal immigrants, the DREAM Act and its narratives of American identity, and the Define American website and project created by illegal immigrant activist José Antonio Vargas. In all those ways, and many others, public American Studies scholarship and conversations impact our present and future just as much as our understanding of our past and identity.*

Keywords: Chinese Exclusion Act; DefineAmerican.com; Deportation policies; DREAM Act; José Antonio Vargas; Obama administration

Railton, Ben. *The Chinese Exclusion Act: What It Can Teach Us about America.* New York: Palgrave Macmillan, 2013. DOI: 10.1057/9781137339096.

It's without a doubt the central question for all of us who seek to produce public American Studies scholarship, to bring our perspectives on and analyses of American culture and identity, histories and stories to a broad national audience: so what? What effects will this work have on our contemporary moment, on our ongoing conversations and debates, on our identities and communities in the present and future? Why should 21st century Americans, particularly those who are not naturally interested in history per se, engage with these topics?

We academic scholars, and perhaps especially academic historians, tend to couch our work in familiar and comfortable narratives of objectivity and analysis, of avoiding presentist or political purposes in favor of doing right by the histories we're studying. I certainly agree that our first responsibility is indeed to be as accurate to and analytical toward those histories as possible, and that we fail utterly if we cherry-pick or over-simplify or (worst of all) misrepresent the past in order to serve a present or political agenda. As I noted in the Introduction, that's what differentiates our work from that of the partisan pundits and propagandists, and we can't lose that distinction without losing the reasons why our voices and work represent something stronger and more exemplary. Yet I also believe that it's far from an either-or proposition: that we can do responsible, accurate, and analytical scholarly work on historical topics and still find ways to connect that work to the present, to argue for its continuing value and meaning in our contemporary moment and culture. And frankly, I believe it's vitally important for us to make that argument: because it makes clear that our work is just as (if not more) meaningful outside of academic conversations as it is inside them; because too many of the voices currently dominating our national conversations and debates have (at best) a deeply simplified sense of our past and culture[1]; and, most significantly, because it's *true*.

That truth, that we have much to learn from history for our own moment, is often presented through the clichéd saying "Those who forget the past are doomed to repeat it." To me, that idea isn't problematic because it's become a cliché, but because it misses the point, and in fact reinforces the aforementioned concerns about presentism in historical analysis. The present isn't the same as the past, and couldn't be—every context, every element, every aspect of a past moment or era is specific, distinct, and its own; the more we anachronistically read our own moment or era back into history, the less possible it is to do that

DOI: 10.1057/9781137339096

responsible and analytical scholarly work, to understand history with any accuracy or complexity. The key, then, is to move in the other direction: to see how, once we've begun to learn about and engage with the past, we can bring our ensuing knowledge and analyses and perspectives to bear on the present, how they can help us similarly engage with and analyze our own specific, distinct, and evolving moment and era. And if we can do that, then we can indeed do the one thing that the clichéd saying gets absolutely right: impact the future and help create an American identity and community that are more complex and stronger, more engaged, and more unified, as a result of these efforts.

I believe there would be lots of ways to bring the histories and analyses for which I've argued in this book to bear on our own present moment, but want to conclude by highlighting two particularly complex and salient such contemporary connections. In keeping with my dual tones and emphases in this book, the first represents one of the darkest and most divisive (in every sense) aspects of early 21st century American politics and society, while the second (despite being similarly controversial and hotly debated) can connect us to some of our most inspiring American lives and identities. But our conversations about both, again, would benefit greatly from broader awareness of and engagement with the histories and stories I've highlighted and analyzed here.

The first connection is to our federal government's increasingly aggressive and destructive deportation policies for undocumented and illegal immigrants. While Arizona's controversial and overtly discriminatory S.B. 1070 and subsequent laws related to illegal immigration in other states have garnered much of the national attention over the last few years—and while certainly our debates over those laws and issues would likewise be significantly shifted with the kinds of historical awareness and analysis for which I've argued here—it's fair to say that the Obama administration's deportation policies have had at least as profound, and more broadly dispersed, effects on American individuals, families, and communities. The number of annual deportations—which is officially divided into two categories, "removals" (forced deportation), and "returns" (ostensibly voluntary departures, although these too tend to be connected to federal actions)—has steadily risen for most of the last two decades; but in 2010 and 2011 that total both significantly increased overall and, according to an April 2012 Immigration and Customs Enforcement (ICE) report, included significant numbers of parents with children who are U.S. citizens.[2]

DOI: 10.1057/9781137339096

That report and those numbers are of course hugely complex, contested in many ways, and connected to multiple contexts that would require extensive investigation. For example, both the ICE and Department of Homeland Security Secretary Janet Napolitano have argued that many of the parents deported had been convicted of crimes, and were indeed often "repeat offenders and fugitives" (although that too is a complex argument, since the ICE report did not specify what crimes had been committed, and they could ironically include the lack of documentation itself). Yet neither Napolitano nor any other official or commentator has disputed the fact that many of those individuals deported over the last few years have been parents, that their children have generally been born in the United States and so have not been similarly deported, and thus that the policy has divided families in a variety of unquestionable ways. And I have my own clear, if anecdotal, evidence for that fact, as my mother works with numerous such families as part of the Bright Stars preschool program in Virginia and has seen many parents (particularly fathers) deported away from their spouses and/or children.

Given that human element to these deportations, it might seem as if the key question to determine one's position on this policy would be that of empathy: whether we can imagine ourselves in this situation, and how that would inform our attitude toward it. But I don't think that's at all fair to proponents of deportation, and I would instead argue for another crucial determining factor: our understanding of the histories of legal and illegal immigration. For those Americans who believe that those categories have been relatively constant or stable throughout our history—those who would claim, to go back to where I began Chapter 1, that "my ancestors came here legally"—applying the full force of the law to illegal immigrants is a perfectly logical, and perhaps the only rational, response. During his campaign for the 2012 Republican presidential nomination, former Pennsylvania Senator Rick Santorum said of illegal immigrants that they don't just break the law, they break it every day—and for those Americans who believe that throughout our history, immigration has represented a consistent and fundamental choice between following and breaking the law (and again that their own ancestors chose to follow it), the dichotomy between those legal immigrants and contemporary illegal ones can seem so blatant as to render empathy impossible or irrelevant.

If we can recognize instead just how much the categories of legal and illegal have been constructed, how recently those constructions have taken place, and just as significantly how fully those constructions have been influenced in each stage of their evolution by explicitly discriminatory definitions and divisions, then our attitudes and arguments can and must shift as well. After all, what the histories I traced in Chapter 1 reveal most centrally is that neither "legal immigrant" nor "illegal immigrant" has much genuine meaning at all; for centuries they had none, and for the last century or so they have existed in a profoundly contingent way, dependent on prevailing cultural attitudes and institutionalized xenophobia and wartime reversals and many other factors. That understanding wouldn't change our current laws or their potential applications, necessarily—but it would at least force us to look more closely at contemporary immigrants (legal, illegal, undocumented) and to consider our own historical and cultural contingencies, the factors that have contributed to our categories and definitions. That kind of empathy, a historical and cultural and legal kind that connects contemporary American communities to those throughout our past, is both more nuanced than a simple human connection (powerful as the latter can be) and more supportable through argument and analysis, and comprises to my mind an important way to fold this current issue and debate into long-term American histories and identities.

Many of the same contexts and connections would inform our debates over the second contemporary issue I want to highlight here, the DREAM Act: the proposed (but so far not passed) Congressional bill that would allow Americans who came to the country illegally as children to become eligible to apply for citizenship if they complete a college degree or serve in the armed forces.[3] Certainly those more accurate understandings of immigration history, and especially of legal and illegal immigration, would again lead to a different perspective on the Americans affected by this potential law. It was in explicit opposition to the DREAM Act, for example, that Sarah Palin expressed her version of the mythologized narrative of past legal immigration, the Ellis Island speech with which I began Chapter 1. But in this case, I would likewise argue that my Chapter 2 focal points, the popular and prominent narratives of American diversity and the more accurate and longstanding histories they elide, could significantly inform our perspectives as well.

After all, the most famous supporter of, and indeed candidate for, the DREAM Act would have to be José Antonio Vargas, the journalist and self-identified illegal immigrant whose story, website, and "Define American" project I discussed in Chapter 2. As I noted there, Vargas explicitly links his own experiences, the ways in which he hopes to redefine "American," and the identities of many (if not all) of those affected by the DREAM Act to the idea of the "fourth wave of immigration that began in 1965" and has "forever changed the ethnic make-up of our country." While it is of course literally true that the DREAM Act would only affect such recent immigrants, Vargas' definitions here go further, and as I argued there overtly parallel the arguments of anti-immigration and diversity activists like Pat Buchanan: for both of these sides, that is, the DREAM Act and contemporary illegal immigrants are pieces of a larger set of changes in America, exemplifications of how American identity and community are different today than what they were in our past. And to my mind, portraying contemporary illegal immigrants, including those who would be eligible for the DREAM Act, as different from past immigrants (in any category) plays directly into the hands of those like Buchanan who likewise want to identify such differences (if for diametrically opposed reasons): in immigrants who refuse to assimilate, in a multiculturally divided society, in an America that has lost its founding and defining characteristics and unity.

On the other hand, if we better remember and engage with the histories and stories of American diversity for which I argued in Chapters 2 and 3, these narratives once again significantly shift. For one thing, many contemporary illegal immigrants (including many who have been highlighted as exemplary DREAM Act candidates) came to the United States from Mexico and other Latin American nations; if we remember the multicentury history of Spanish and Mexican American settlement, community, and identity, as well as the ways in which those communities were far too often dispossessed (both of their homes and of their place in our national histories), it becomes much harder to see these 21st century Americans as anything other than descendants of foundational national communities. And for another, even more overarching thing, stories like Vargas' resonate quite directly and powerfully with those of the Angel Island poets, Yung Wing, and the Chinese Educational Mission students: all of whom were at crucial moments in their own lives illegal immigrants, defined as outside of our national community, unable to enter and required to leave America; yet all of whom represent and embody instead some of the best of what American identity and ideals have been and can be. I would say precisely the same of José Antonio Vargas and his peers—and being able to see them as another chapter in an originating and ongoing American story makes it much easier to define them not

DOI: 10.1057/9781137339096

as illegal immigrants but as inspiring and vital members of our national community.

Remembering these lessons of the Chinese Exclusion Act certainly helps us better understand and engage with our past: with what it hasn't actually included (despite many of our most enduring narratives) and what it has, who we've always been and who we haven't (despite some of our most familiar definitions). But it also and even more significantly helps us better understand our contemporary society, not only in terms of these particular issues and debates but at our core. These memories can teach us to see that much of what most clearly defines us today, our immigrant, multicultural, and diverse populace, represents a direct through-line to what has defined us throughout our history. They can help us recognize that the narratives that push back on those defining qualities do so in large part by constructing and echoing over-simplified and mythologized visions of our past and identity. And, perhaps most importantly, they can offer us new and inspiring American histories and stories, powerful identities and communities that exemplify what America has always been and can be even more fully in the century to come.

Notes

1 Perhaps the best example I can cite is one I mentioned in the Introduction: Glenn Beck's Beck University, the online, for-profit "educational" institution that presents itself quite explicitly as public scholarship from which all Americans can and should learn. Beck University's motto is "Learn History as It Really Happened"; but its "American" expert is David Barton, the minister and pundit best known for his profoundly inaccurate arguments that the Founding Fathers intended America to be a Christian nation.

2 For official year-by-year statistics on both removals and returns, see for example http://econlog.econlib.org/archives/2011/08/deportations_st.html. For more on the ICE report, see *USA Today* story: http://www.usatoday.com/USCP/PNI/Front%20Page/2012-04-05-pni0405met-parents-deportedPNIBrd_ST_U.htm.

3 In June 2012, President Obama issued an Executive Order that, while not providing such a path to citizenship, exempted certain such young Americans from the threat of deportation. Controversial as the Order was and is, particularly among opponents of the DREAM Act, it remains a very partial and preliminary step, and does not resolve any of the questions with which I am concerned here.

DOI: 10.1057/9781137339096

A Few Suggestions for Further Reading

For each of my chapters and main focal points, there are many more significant and strong scholarly books than I'd be able to cite or engage with in notes. I can't do anything like justice to those lists here either, but I hope that these at least provide some strong starting points for further reading.

Chapter 1 What the Act Can Teach Us about Immigration History and Laws

Daniels, Roger. *Guarding the Golden Door: American Immigration Policy and Immigrants since 1882*. New York: Hill and Wang, 2004.

Gerber, David. *American Immigration: A Very Short Introduction*. Oxford: Oxford University Press, 2011.

Hing, Bill Ong. *Defining America through Immigration Policy*. Philadelphia: Temple University Press, 2004.

Lau, Estelle. *Paper Families: Identity, Immigration Administration, and Chinese Exclusion*. Durham: Duke University Press, 2006.

LeMay, Michael. *From Open Door to Dutch Door: An Analysis of U.S. Immigration Policy since 1820*. New York: Praeger, 1987.

Moloney, Deirdre. *National Insecurities: Immigrants and U.S. Deportation Policy since 1882*. Chapel Hill: University of North Carolina Press, 2012.

DOI: 10.1057/9781137339096

Salyer, Lucy Elizabeth. *Guarding the "White Man's Frontier": Courts, Politics, and the Regulation of Immigration, 1891–1924*. PhD Thesis, University of California, Berkeley, 1989.
Soennichsen, John Robert. *The Chinese Exclusion Act of 1882*. Santa Barbara, CA: Greenwood, 2011.

Chapter 2 What the Act Can Teach Us about Diversity

Behdad, Ali. *A Forgetful Nation: On Immigration and Cultural Identity in the United States*. Durham: Duke University Press, 2005.
Buisseret, David and Steven G. Reinhardt, eds. *Creolization in the Americas*. College Station: Texas A&M University Press, 2000.
Frederickson, George. *Diverse Nations: Explorations in the History of Racial and Ethnic Pluralism*. Boulder: Paradigm, 2008.
Iceland, John. *Where We Live Now: Immigration and Race in the United States*. Berkeley: University of California Press, 2009.
King, Desmond. *Making Americans: Immigration, Race, and the Origins of the Diverse Democracy*. Cambridge: Harvard University Press, 2000.
Railton, Ben. *Redefining American Identity: From Cabeza de Vaca to Barack Obama*. New York: Palgrave Macmillan, 2011.
Rosenwald, Lawrence. *Multilingual America: Language and the Making of American Literature*. Cambridge: Cambridge University Press, 2008.
Sollors, Werner, ed. *Multilingual America: Transnationalism, Ethnicity, and the Languages of American Literature*. New York: New York University Press, 1998.
Takaki, Ronald. *A Different Mirror: A History of Multicultural America*. Boston: Little, Brown, 1993.

Chapter 3 What the Act Can Teach Us about Forgotten and Inspiring American Stories

Hing, Bill Ong. *Making and Remaking Asian America through Immigration Policy, 1850–1990*. Stanford: Stanford University Press, 1993.
Hsu, Francis L.K. *Americans and Chinese: Passage to Differences*. 3rd edition. Honolulu: University of Hawaii Press, 1981.

DOI: 10.1057/9781137339096

La Fargue, Thomas E. *China's First Hundred: Educational Mission Students in the United States, 1872–1881*. Pullman, WA: Washington State University Press, 1987.

Leibovitz, Leil and Matthew Miller. *Fortunate Sons: The 120 Chinese Boys Who Came to America, Went to School, and Revolutionized an Ancient Civilization*. New York: Norton, 2011.

Palumbo-Liu, David. *Asian/America: Historical Crossings of a Racial Frontier*. Stanford: Stanford University Press, 1999.

Peffer, George Anthony. *If They Don't Bring Their Women Here: Chinese Female Immigration before Exclusion*. Urbana: University of Illinois Press, 1999.

Rhoads, Edward J.M. *Stepping Forth into the World: The Chinese Educational Mission to the United States, 1872–1881*. Hong Kong: Hong Kong University Press, 2011.

Seligman, Scott. *The First Chinese American: The Remarkable Life of Wong Chin Foo*. Hong Kong: Hong Kong University Press, 2013.

DOI: 10.1057/9781137339096

Index

DOI: 10.1057/9781137339096

DOI: 10.1057/9781137339096

CPSIA information can be obtained at www.ICGtesting.com
Printed in the USA
LVOW13*0218100214

373028LV00004B/41/P

9 781137 339089